PRESENTED TO:

―――――――――――――――――――――――

BY:

―――――――――――――――――――――――

DATE:

―――――――――――――――――――――――

GOOD NIGHT, GOD!

HONOR
BOOKS

07 06 05 04 03   10 9 8 7 6 5 4 3 2 1

Good Night, God!
Nighttime Devotions to End Your Day God's Way
ISBN 1-56292-302-1
Copyright © 2003 by Honor Books,
An Imprint of Cook Communications Ministries
4050 Lee Vance View
Colorado Springs, CO 80918

Developed by Bordon Books

Good Night, God!

Nighttime Devotions to End Your Day God's Way

❧ INTRODUCTION ❧

All day long you completed tasks and went about your daily duties while He waited and watched over you. He looked for your acknowledgement of His presence throughout the day. He loves you. He can't get enough of your company. He has special secrets about the way He designed life—your life—that He wants to let you in on. As you prepare to retire for the evening, take a few moments to tell Him about your day. *But how should I start*, you ask?

We often reflect on the challenges of the day as the evening draws to a close. We know that time with God can really make rest complete and meaningful. Yet sometimes the stress of the day leaves us eager for our heads to hit the pillow. How can we find time for God?

Good Night, God! is a collection of short meditations and stories to make it possible to fit a quiet, life-changing moment into your evening. Read the short entry and the Bible verse. Think about the nudges you feel in your heart—you know, the ones you feel when God speaks to you. Talk to Him about those nudges. It won't take long, and that precious time will bring sweet rest and comfort to your evening.

A PICTURE OF HOPE

While visiting relatives in a rural area, a father decided to take his young daughter for an evening walk along a country road. The family lived in a large city, where walking at night was not the custom or considered safe. The father could hardly wait to see how his daughter would respond to a star-filled sky.

At first, his daughter was playful, exploring the flowers and insects along the edge of the dirt lane. As dusk turned into dark, however, she became a little fearful and clung to his hand tightly. She seemed grateful for the flashlight he had brought along. Suddenly, she looked toward the sky and exclaimed with surprise, "Daddy, somebody drew dots all over the sky!"

Her father smiled. His young daughter had never seen a night sky away from the city lights. He was glad the moon had not yet risen and the stars appeared even closer and more distinct. "Daddy," she continued in her enthusiasm, "if we connect them all, will they make a picture?"

The night sky had taken on the quality of a dot-to-dot puzzle for his child! *What an interesting notion,* the father thought. "No," he replied to his daughter, "the dots are there for another purpose. Each one is a hope God has for your life. God loves you so much.

He has lots of hopes that your life will be filled with good things. In fact, there are more hopes than you or I can ever count!"

"I knew it!" the little girl gasped. "The dots *do* make a picture." And then she added more thoughtfully, "I always wondered what hope looked like."

When God showed Abraham the stars and asked Him to count them, He was giving him hope that the promise He had made to him—that he would have a son—was coming.

Whenever the sky is clear at night, do some stargazing! The stars are a picture of God's hope—for you, for your family, for the world. Stargazing is one of the best ways to get your earthly life back into perspective and realize that, in God's infinite universe, He has a specific plan for you, just as He did for Abraham.

━━━━

THEN HE BROUGHT HIM [ABRAHAM] OUTSIDE AND SAID, "LOOK NOW TOWARD HEAVEN, AND COUNT THE STARS IF YOU ARE ABLE TO NUMBER THEM." AND HE SAID TO HIM, "SO SHALL YOUR DESCENDANTS BE."

GENESIS 15:5 NKJV

↬ GOD'S MASTERPIECE ↬

As you lie in bed tonight, stretch your limbs in all
directions and then relax for a moment to ponder the
fact that your body has been fearfully and wonderfully
made. The word "fearfully" in this context is like the
word of supreme quality that has been popular among
teens in recent years, "Awesome!"

When you stop to think about all the intricate
details involved in the normal functioning of your
body—just one creation among countless species and
organisms on the planet—you must conclude, "The
Designer of this piece of work had a marvelous plan."

Listen to your heartbeat. Flex your fingers and
toes. Keep in mind as you do that:

↬ *No one else among all humanity has your exact*
   fingerprints, handprint, or footprint.
↬ *No one else has your voiceprint.*
↬ *No one else has your genetic code—the exact*
   positioning of the many genes that define your
   physical characteristics.

Furthermore, no one else has your exact history
in time and space. No one else has gone where you've

gone, done what you've done, said what you've said, or created what you've created. You are truly a one-of-a-kind masterpiece.

The Lord knows precisely *how* you were made and *why* you were made. When something in your life goes amiss, He knows how to fix it. When you err or stray from His commandments, He knows how to woo you back and work even the worst tragedies and mistakes for your good when you repent.

You have been uniquely fashioned for a specific purpose on the earth. He has a "design" for your life. It is His own imprint, His own mark. Make a resolution in these night hours to be true to what the Lord has made you to be and to become.

I WILL PRAISE THEE;
FOR I AM FEARFULLY AND
WONDERFULLY MADE: MARVELOUS
ARE THY WORKS; AND THAT
MY SOUL KNOWETH RIGHT WELL.

PSALM 139:14 KJV

↢ UNEXPECTED ANGELS ↢

Kathleen Lowthert described a special conversation she had with her granddaughter at a critical time in Kathleen's life.

Kathleen, who was scheduled to have an operation several days later, was joined by two-year-old Shanice one day as she was having her daily devotions. After reading her Bible and praying, Kathleen began reading some information about the anesthesia she would receive prior to surgery. The more she read, the more she realized how nervous she was about the operation.

That's when Shanice looked at her and said, "Grandmom, show me the angels."

"Angels?" Kathleen asked.

Then Shanice pointed to a photo on the cover of the brochure Kathleen had been reading. "No, Honey," Kathleen said. "That's a doctor, a nurse, and a patient."

"Yes, Grandmom—angels," Shanice replied.

Her granddaughter's simple misunderstanding proved to be a powerful reminder to Kathleen that God would indeed give His angels charge over her. She decided right then that she would not waste another moment worrying about the operation. Peace

↢

flooded over her as she thanked God for the protection she knew He would provide during her stay in the hospital.[1]

Kathleen vividly saw how children can remind us of the simplest truths. There are times in all of our lives when we worry about our families, health, finances, job, and the many decisions that we may have to make on a regular basis. We spend more time worrying about the problem than taking steps to solve it. Are you unable to sleep because you can't stop thinking about your problems? It's time to take that next big step.

Put yourself in God's hands tonight and pray that He will lead you in the right direction. Then simply let go and trust Him, believing that you will sense God's direction and that He will bring you the peace you need.

═══════

HE WILL COMMAND HIS
ANGELS CONCERNING YOU TO
GUARD YOU IN ALL YOUR WAYS.

PSALM 91:11

❧ PEACE IN THE STORM ❧

Our darkest hour is often the prelude to a great victory. God invades our circumstances and hides us with His cloak.

Late in the night on Monday, August 24, 1992, America's most destructive hurricane, Andrew, slammed into the east coast of Florida near Miami. Fierce winds, measuring up to 164 miles an hour, blasted a path of destruction across the peninsula. Andrew's fury left behind broken glass, buckled doors, split ceilings, roofs ripped from the walls, and soaked furniture blown blocks away.

Many who stayed to face the worst of the raging winds hid in small, windowless bathrooms, with entire families shielded by mattresses, hoping the storm would spare them. Those who evacuated returned only to wonder where they were. "It was horrible," Jeanette said, reliving the pain. "I couldn't find my house in all the wreckage. Nothing was recognizable. It looked like a nuclear weapon had hit."

A veil of darkness and fear fell upon Jeanette and her family. Facing the shock of Andrew's damage, they realized the awesome power of this natural disaster. After experiencing the trauma of the storm itself, they found that day-to-day life was becoming increasingly difficult. It was in the midst of this fury that God moved in. "Left with only the clothes on our backs, we knew God had saved us. We refused to be beaten, and God gave us the strength and courage to not give up," Jeanette said.

In this seemingly hopeless situation for Jeanette's family, God flooded their lives by meeting all of their needs. "The Lord provided for us in miraculous ways, and every day became brighter," Jeanette recalled.

Many people are faced with situations like Jeanette's, such as the devastation left behind by natural disasters like floods, tornadoes, and hurricanes. If you are one of those, ask the Lord to flood the darkness with His light. As the raging storms swirl around you, God will burst forth with the light of His presence.

HE MADE DARKNESS HIS SECRET PLACE; HIS PAVILION ROUND ABOUT HIM WERE DARK WATERS AND THICK CLOUDS OF THE SKIES.

PSALM 18:11 KJV

↭ SAVING TIME? ↭

Modern timesaving appliances and devices give us the opportunity to make choices about how to use our time. We can spend less time doing things we *don't* enjoy in order to have more time to *do* the things we do enjoy. But what is it we enjoy doing?

Twenty-year-old college student Amy Wu wrote about her aunt who "tends her house as if it were her child." The house is spotlessly clean. Smells of home-cooked meals drift through the house. Roses from the garden are artfully arranged in beautiful vases. Her aunt can afford a housekeeper, but she enjoys doing her own housework.

Amy went on, "I'm a failure at housework. I've chosen to be inept and unlearned at what my aunt has spent so much time perfecting. At 13, I avoided domestic chores as my contribution to the women's movement. Up to now, I've thought there were more important things to do."

But those "more important things" didn't turn out to be all that important. She explained, "It isn't as if we're using the time we save for worthwhile pursuits. . . . Most of my friends spend the extra minutes watching TV, listening to stereos, shopping, hanging out, chatting on the phone, or snoozing."

↭

One day she decided to make a meal for her family. While the dinner was cooking, she wrote a letter to her cousin. Then she made a chocolate cake to celebrate her sister's birthday. It was a success. "That night I grinned as my father and sister dug into the pasta, then the cake, licking their lips in appreciation. It had been a long time since I'd felt so proud. A week later my cousin called and thanked me for my letter, the first handwritten correspondence she'd received in two years."

She concluded, "Sure, my generation has all the technological advances at our fingertips. We're computer savvy, and we have more time. But what are we really saving it for? In the end, we may lose more than we've gained by forgetting the important things in life."[2]

How do you spend your elective time? Like Amy's friends, or caring for family and growing closer to the Lord?

IN ALL YOUR GETTING,
GET UNDERSTANDING.

PROVERBS 4:7 NKJV

↭ THINGS THAT GO BUMP ↭

I'm going to be brave tonight, the eight-year-old told herself as she was getting ready for bed. *I am going to sleep in the dark whether I'm afraid or not.*

For several months she had tried to accept the darkness without fear, but night after night "the things that go bump" got louder and louder.

As Emily crawled under the covers, her eyes were as big as saucers. Darkness filled every corner of her room. She was determined not to be afraid, until all at once she heard that bump. She jumped up, wondering what was in her room that had caused all that commotion.

"I knew it was going to happen!" she cried out.

Emily jumped up and switched on her night-light, revealing her familiar toys and dolls. She returned to bed with a lighter heart and a sense of peace and fell asleep right away. There's something comforting about the light that chases away fear from a child's mind.

Being in physical darkness is not pleasant. But one thing that's worse is living an entire lifetime in spiritual darkness without the love and

↭

companionship of Jesus Christ. Without Him, the sun doesn't shine brightly enough, and the stars aren't as special as they twinkle in the heavens above us. Without Him, the world is a lonely and desolate place, filled with things that go bump in the night.

When Christ enters the heart of man, a transformation takes place immediately. The shadows lift, and a new joy replaces the fear that once possessed the soul. The night doesn't frighten us anymore. Knowing He's in control provides peace and contentment.

I WILL LIE DOWN AND SLEEP IN
PEACE, FOR YOU ALONE, O LORD,
MAKE ME DWELL IN SAFETY.

PSALM 4:8

❧ LIVING WONDERFULLY ❧

We all know the story of the movie *It's a Wonderful Life*. George Bailey's Uncle Billy loses $8,000 on the day the bank examiner shows up, and George is frantic. In despair, he goes home and looks at his house and family with discouraged eyes. He decides he is a failure at business, one of his children is sick, his house is all but coming down around his ears—why not just put an end to his life?

Thank God for Clarence! Through a series of events, this angel without wings shows George how much his life has meant to his family and friends. Without George, his brother Harry would be dead; Mr. Gower, the druggist, would be in prison; his wife would be a frightened old maid; and Bedford Falls would be known as Pottersville—a town as mean and miserable as its namesake.

When George Bailey took an honest look at his life, he could see that despite all the disappointments there were more than enough triumphs to balance the scales. He had done the best he could, and that had brought tremendous blessings to his family, friends, and community.

❧

At the end of the movie, George's brother calls him "the richest man in town," and he was—in all the ways that really matter.

Have you had a similar crisis of conscience, a moment when you wondered if your life was worth anything? Take note of these words from Bishop Thomas Wilson (1663-1755), and ask yourself these questions at the close of each day:

↬ *What good am I doing in the world?*

↬ *Am I bringing up my children to fear God?*

↬ *Have I been kind and helpful to poor and needy people?*

↬ *Have I been honest in all my dealings?*

↬ *Have I lived in the fear of God and worshipped Him both publicly and privately?*[3]

The wisest thing to do is keep short accounts. Take stock of your life often. Don't wait for the closing chapter to decide how your book will end!

WHEN YOU ARE ON YOUR BEDS,
SEARCH YOUR HEARTS AND BE SILENT.

PSALM 4:4

⊷ LIFESAVING LIGHT ⊷

The day was full of light! The waves tumbled against the shore in a most inviting way, while a slight breeze made the palm trees shudder with delight.

The scuba diving club decided it was a great day for an underwater adventure. Everyone geared up excitedly. After the leader assigned buddies, Jim, a member of the group, was particularly eager because this was his first real dive. He had practiced in small bodies of water many times, but seeing the ocean floor was a dream come true.

After offering a brief goodbye to his family, he walked out into the ocean. Then seemingly out of nowhere, a storm blew in. Pellet-like raindrops fell as thunder crashed. Lightning popped all around. Everyone scattered, seeking shelter. About an hour into the storm, Jim's family panicked. The other divers were returning, but Jim had not been seen anywhere.

His family and friends began to pray. After another half-hour, he came running toward the car through the darkness of the storm. It turned out that when he had returned to the surface of the ocean, the storm was so heavy and the clouds were so dark that he couldn't see the shoreline. So he dropped his gear and swam toward a glowing light, which guided him to safety.

That day Jim learned some important lessons about life and scuba diving. Sometimes when storms break out, a person must be willing to let go of the weights that hold him down. No matter how valuable the scuba gear, Jim's life was more important. He never replaced the equipment but allowed it to rest forever on the ocean floor.

His love for his family and God increased greatly as a result of the dive. He realized, too, that during even the bleakest hours of life, God's light is the light that leads to life.

———

"I AM THE LIGHT OF THE WORLD. WHOEVER FOLLOWS ME WILL NEVER WALK IN DARKNESS, BUT WILL HAVE THE LIGHT OF LIFE."

JOHN 8:12

ᏕᎢ TWENTY-FOUR SEVEN Ꮥ
FRIENDSHIP

One evening a drug addict admitted during an
Alcoholics Anonymous meeting that he often felt the
need to have a drink in the middle of the night. Mark
had to find a way to keep from drinking, because he
knew his alcoholism was a matter of life and death.
He sought the help of his fellow alcoholics.

"I'm going to pass my phone book around the
room," Mark told the others in the room. "If any
one of you wouldn't mind getting a call from me in
the middle of the night, please jot down your name
and phone number."

Mark emphasized to the attendees that if they
had any misgivings, he didn't want them to put their
phone numbers in his book.

"I want to be able to call you without feeling
guilty," he explained, "and, of course, if you don't
want to be disturbed during the night, I understand
that too. You don't have to sign the book."

As the book circulated throughout the room,
Mark saw people digging into their pockets and
purses for pencils. The room was silent while he
waited for the phone book to be returned to him.

ᏕᎢ

Mark couldn't help but wonder how many people would sign the book.

Moments later, the last man to sign the book handed it to Mark. When Mark opened the book, he began to cry. He discovered he had some really good friends—lots of them.

Fifty-six people were at the meeting. Fifty-six people signed his book.

On his way home, Mark rejoiced, knowing he could receive help at night by calling one of his new friends, people whom God had brought into his life. That kind of friend is a treasure—a blessing to our lives. A friend is one we can call in the midst of our despair, no matter what time of night. And we can be treasures in return by offering a listening ear in the middle of the night.

———

TWO ARE BETTER THAN ONE, BECAUSE THEY HAVE A GOOD REWARD FOR THEIR LABOR. FOR IF THEY FALL, ONE WILL LIFT UP HIS COMPANION. BUT WOE TO HIM WHO IS ALONE WHEN HE FALLS, FOR HE HAS NO ONE TO HELP HIM UP.

ECCLESIASTES 4:9-10 NKJV

↬ IT'S TAKEN CARE OF ↫

Andrea was in no mood for her six-year-old
son's Saturday afternoon antics. While Steven argued
with his friends over video games, Andrea stewed over
her own mounting pile of pressures. Just-bought
groceries for tomorrow's dinner guests sprawled
across every bit of counter space. Buried under them
was a Sunday school lesson to be prepared. A week's
worth of laundry spilled out of the laundry room into
the kitchen, and an upsetting letter from a faraway
friend in need lay teetering on the edge of the sink.

In the midst of this turmoil, Steven's Sunday
school teacher called. "Is Steven going to the carnival
with us this afternoon?"

"He didn't mention anything about it."

"Well, we'll be leaving about five. If he didn't
bring home his permission slip, just write the usual
information on a slip of paper and send it along with
him." As soon as Andrea reminded Steven about the
trip, his mood changed, and he was his "better self"
for the next couple of hours.

Andrea was just pulling a cake from the oven
when she heard the doorbell ring, followed by an

↬↫

awful commotion. Rushing to the living room she found two little girls waving pink slips of paper at her crying son.

"I can't go!" he wailed. "I don't have one of those pink papers!"

"Oh, yes, you do. Only yours happens to be white," she said as she dried his tears, stuffed the paper in his pocket, and sent him out the door.

Back in the kitchen Andrea wondered, *Why didn't he just ask me about the paper? Hasn't he been my child long enough to know I'd have a solution?*

Suddenly a tiny smile crept across her face as she surveyed the chaos around her—and she could almost hear her Heavenly Father say, "Haven't you been My child long enough to know that I have it taken care of?"[4]

═══

"DO NOT LET YOUR HEARTS
BE TROUBLED. TRUST IN GOD;
TRUST ALSO IN ME."

JOHN 14:1

⇥ MICROWAVE FRIENDSHIP ⇤

When Sara was a little girl and went to visit her grandpa, he would set her on the kitchen counter and let her watch him make popcorn in the popcorn machine. Those special times with Grandpa and the popcorn machine were not to last. The problem was not that Sara had grown too big to sit on the counter. Rather, Grandpa discovered the convenience of microwave popcorn. It was easy, cheap, and quick.

Now when Sara visits him, Grandpa asks her to put a bag into the "micro" and "nuke" it. Sara eats the popcorn, but she looks around the kitchen, and there's no Grandpa enjoying it with her. It takes only one person to stick a bag of popcorn into the microwave, and Sara misses those precious moments of making popcorn with him.

Have we become a generation of microwave friends—friends who are here one minute and gone the next, like a fast-food hamburger? We used to call this type of friend an acquaintance—someone we met occasionally in our daily life, someone to have lunch with, meet at the same party, or see a movie with once in a while. It was enjoyable sharing our time with these people, but we knew they were not the friends who would sacrifice themselves to help us in a time of need.

The individual we could count on to assist us and whom we would sacrifice our needs to help in any and all circumstances was our true friend. This was the person we had spent time with, cried with, and rejoiced with—the person we had a history with and had taken the time to discover who they were, what they were like, and what they believed in. This was a person who shared in the same belief system we did. Friendship is a relationship that stays strong no matter what.

God made us to need one another. Cultivate real friendships and weed out the phony ones.[5]

———

THERE ARE "FRIENDS" WHO PRETEND TO BE FRIENDS, BUT THERE IS A FRIEND WHO STICKS CLOSER THAN A BROTHER.

PROVERBS 18:24 TLB

❧ NIGHTTIME · BENEDICTION ❧

A benediction is the pronouncing of a divine blessing. It is usually associated with the final words of a worship service given by a spiritual leader, but you can give yourself a benediction right where you are this very night!

The only requirement for a benediction is this: that no sin or unforgiveness stands between you and the Lord Jesus Christ. If you question the purity of your heart, tonight is a good time to ask the Lord to cleanse you and renew a right spirit within you.

Then face yourself in a mirror before you turn off the lights for the night and pronounce a divine blessing upon yourself. Speak it with faith and boldness, in full confidence that the Lord desires this blessing to take root in you and bear good fruit. If you have a family, you may want to pronounce a blessing on them as a group or on each member individually.

By doing so, you can end each day with a keen awareness of God's blessing and His claim on your life.

The benediction inscribed at Gloucester Cathedral is one you may want to use:

❧

Good Night, GOD!

Go on your way in peace.
Be of good courage.
Hold fast that which is good.
Render to no man evil for evil.
Strengthen the fainthearted.
Support the weak.
Help and cheer the sick.
Honor all men.
Love and serve the Lord.
May the blessing of God be upon you and
   remain with you forever.

So be it. And have a blessed good night.

THE VERY GOD OF PEACE SANCTIFY
YOU WHOLLY; AND I PRAY GOD YOUR
WHOLE SPIRIT AND SOUL AND BODY
BE PRESERVED BLAMELESS UNTO THE
COMING OF OUR LORD JESUS CHRIST.

1 THESSALONIANS 5:23 KJV

❧ NO NIGHT ❧

What is Heaven like?

No doubt most people, if not all, have wondered about that at some point in their lives. Many of us have even turned to the book of Revelation in the Bible to find out what it's like.

Even so, no matter how hard we try, we can't totally comprehend living in a place where night doesn't exist. It's difficult to visualize an environment where there's enough light for everything all the time. In Heaven, we will have no need for electric lights, lamps, flashlights, candles, or even the light of the sun, moon, and stars!

A nightless place where light floods our surroundings at all times is an awesome concept. Yet this is exactly how Heaven is described in the Bible.

Probably most people agree that from what the Bible says, Heaven sounds like a great place to live. Besides no night, the Bible says there won't be any tears, pain, or suffering in Heaven. Instead, all of us will experience joy, peace, and comfort in addition to beautiful mansions, gold streets, and sparkling jewels.

At times, we may think that such a place sounds too good to be true. We may wonder, *What's the catch?*

❧

The good news is, there is no catch. God has promised that we will have the opportunity to spend eternity in a state of happiness in Heaven—if we will believe in His Son, Jesus.

Tonight, reflect on Heaven and the happiness we're bound to receive when we get there. Think about seeing your friends and relatives in Heaven without having to struggle through any painful arguments and quarrels that lead to hurt feelings. We simply won't have any grudges to hold. We will live in harmony with everyone. There will be no need for soldiers to have to go to war because everyone will be at total peace with each other.

What could be a more beautiful thought for us this evening?

THERE WILL BE NO MORE NIGHT.
THEY WILL NOT NEED THE LIGHT
OF A LAMP OR THE LIGHT OF
THE SUN, FOR THE LORD GOD
WILL GIVE THEM LIGHT. AND THEY
WILL REIGN FOR EVER AND EVER.

REVELATION 22:5

❧ THE BEAUTY OF A SUNSET ❧

F. W. Boreham tells the story in *Boulevards of Paradise* of an elderly man taking a walk with his granddaughter. They met a man who poured out to them a long story of the difficulties of his life. He then apologized, explaining that he was suffering from a slight sunstroke.

As the grandfather and his little granddaughter departed, the little girl exclaimed, "Grandpa, I do hope that you will never suffer from a sunset!"

John Lloyd Ogilvie makes an important observation from this tender scene. He writes, "The point is all too clear. We suffer from a sunset before the day is ended. This is not only true for people who give up the adventure of growing spiritually and intellectually in the 'sunset' years of their lives, but also for Christians of every age who stop adventuring with Christ. . . . We can be spiritually geriatric in our twenties or forties!"[6]

Wise sages have given us the perspective on aging:

↔ *"You are as young as your faith, as old as your doubt; as young as your self-confidence, as old as your fear; as young as your hope, as old as your despair."*

↔ *"In the central place of every heart there is a recording chamber. So long as it receives messages of beauty, hope, cheer, and courage—so long are you young."*

❧

↔ *"When your heart is covered with the snows of
pessimism and the ice of cynicism, then and only
then are you grown old."*[7]

We should think of the glorious colors and
magnificence of the sunsets we have seen as we
approach the "sunset" times of our lives—the end of a
day, a project, a journey, or some other significant
season of life.

Sunset is a time of reflection. In nature, a
sunset brings a brilliant and satisfying splendor to
our souls *every day*. Spiritually, sunset is the time we
pause to meditate on God's awesome creation, both
around us and inside of us *every day*.

Every evening you have the opportunity, take time
to view with wonder the spectacular event we know as a
sunset. This is your Heavenly Father's gift to you,
filling you with gratitude for a day well spent with
Him, the sweet sleep He will now give to you, and the
hope and expectancy of spending tomorrow with Him.

MAY THE GOD OF HOPE FILL YOU WITH
ALL JOY AND PEACE IN BELIEVING.

ROMANS 15:13 NASB

STARGAZING

Remember when you were a child, lying on your back outdoors, staring up at the celestial stream of stars and moon? All was peaceful and still. How relaxing it was to quietly gaze at the shimmering lights and simply dream! Even as an adult, you are not too old for that. Everyone needs a quiet time to be alone with God, without television, radio, or teaching tapes. If you can't find quiet time, it's because you've given it away. But you can take it back now.

God created you more special than all other things, even the stars in heaven. The psalmist wrote in Psalm 8:3-5 KJV, "When I consider thy heavens, the work of thy fingers, the moon and the stars, which thou hast ordained; What is man, that thou art mindful of him? And the son of man, that thou visitest him? For thou hast made him a little lower than the angels, and hast crowned him with glory and honour."

God has a special place in His heart just for you, and He wants you to know Him in a more intimate way. The Lord desires this relationship even more than you do. Having your friendship pleases Him.

Don't listen to the lies of the enemy, who tells you that God is angry because you haven't read your Bible lately. As you spend time with God, you will be strengthened. This strength will keep you from throwing in the towel when times get tough. Make your quiet time top priority. Consider it an appointment with God. Mark on your calendar now the time you plan to spend with God each day and give it first place.

─────

THE HEAVENS DECLARE THE GLORY OF GOD; AND THE FIRMAMENT SHEWETH HIS HANDIWORK.

PSALM 19:1 KJV

↜ THE LIGHT OF LIFE ↜

Dwight L. Moody used to tell this story about darkness and light.

"There was a terrible storm one night on Lake Erie. The captain of a ship could see the light from a lighthouse, but, not seeing the lower lights of the harbor, he questioned his pilot about their location.

"'Yes, sir, this is Cleveland,' the pilot said. 'The lower lights have gone out, sir.'

"'Will we make it into the harbor?'

"'If we don't, we're lost, sir,' the pilot replied.

"'The pilot did his best, but it wasn't enough. Without the lower lights to guide them in, the ship crashed on the rocks."

Light is crucial if we want to get to our destination without mishap or error, especially if we want to reach the height of all we believe to be our destiny. Sometimes we might be tempted to try and fight our way through the darkness to prove we're smart enough or tough enough to sail through anything on our own. At other moments, courage fails us and fear blinds us to the light that's right in front of us.

↜

Instead of trying to go on alone, or closing our eyes, we must realize there's a Light available to all of us. This light is guaranteed to guide us through darkness, fog, storms, and anything else that might hinder our progress.

Jesus Christ said, "'I am the Light of the world. Whoever follows me will never walk in darkness, but will have the light of life'" (John 8:12).

As you climb into bed and turn out the lights tonight, remind yourself that the Light within you never dims or goes out. Keep your eyes focused on Jesus, and you will have a safe trip into the harbor!

GOD IS LIGHT AND IN HIM
IS NO DARKNESS AT ALL.

1 JOHN 1:5 NKJV

❧ RAINY DAYS ❧

It was one of those wet rainy days at the end of winter, in that interlude between the cold weather and the warmth of spring, a time of daffodils peeking their bright yellow blossoms through the ground and offering promise of more to come.

In a small house on the corner, Rhonda, a young mother of three, was fixing lunch for her children. Their favorite sandwich was peanut butter and jelly. She took the bread and peanut butter out of the cabinet and removed the blackberry jelly from the refrigerator. The lid on the jar of peanut butter seemed to be stuck tight. She tried and tried to open it, but the lid wouldn't budge.

Suddenly, Rhonda burst into tears. She had reached her limit. The baby had cried all night with colic, so she had gotten little rest; the two-year-old was his usual "terrible twos" self; the rain meant the kids couldn't play outside, and now the dumb lid to the peanut butter jar wouldn't come off.

About that time, her five-year-old daughter came into the kitchen. Kylie had been playing with dolls in her bedroom when she heard her mother crying. The little girl hugged her mother around her waist and said, "Don't cry, Mommy. God will bring the sunshine back tomorrow."

Kylie's words put everything back into perspective for Rhonda. She knew that she had overreacted because she was so tired. Kylie was right. Tomorrow was another day.

Most of us can probably put ourselves in this young mother's place. We've all felt we were at the end of our rope at some time or other. Sometimes the smallest incident causes us to spill over, making us believe we can't cope anymore. Whatever the situation, always remember that God—in the words of a small child—will bring the sunshine back tomorrow.

———

THE LORD GIVES STRENGTH
TO HIS PEOPLE; THE LORD
BLESSES HIS PEOPLE WITH PEACE.

PSALM 29:11

✢ BLESSED SLEEP ✢

"Take two aspirins and call me in the morning."
What is a doctor really saying when he gives you that
instruction? In a way he's saying, "Get a good night's
sleep and see if you don't feel better in the
morning." It's amazing how well that works! Very
often, we do feel better the next morning.

Scientific research supports that theory. In one
study, laboratory rats died of fatal blood infections
after being deprived of sleep for long periods of
time—possibly because their immune systems failed.

Have you ever spent a few nights in a hospital,
specifically in the intensive care unit? A patient's
common complaint might be, "How am I supposed to
get well when they keep waking me up every few
hours?" Good point.

The frequent wake-ups, the noise, and the lights
are believed to contribute to a slower rate of
recovery. In fact, some patients wind up with ICU
syndrome: hallucinations, disorientation, and
depression that all strike after about three days in the
unit. The cause? Probably lack of sleep.

✢

Being stubborn human beings, most of us ignore the bed-rest portion of a doctor's prescription when we have a less serious ailment, such as a cold or the flu. As long as we have to stay home, why not get something done? After all, we aren't dying.

Too often, however, a minor illness becomes something major, and then we have to take to our beds. How much time and trouble could have been saved if we had followed our doctor's orders to begin with? How much healthier would we be if we worked with our immune systems instead of against them?[8]

Writer Aldous Huxley has said, "That we are not much sicker and much madder than we are is due exclusively to that most blessed and blessing of all natural graces, sleep."

Sleep. Enjoy every minute of it!

IN VAIN YOU RISE EARLY AND STAY UP LATE, TOILING FOR FOOD TO EAT—FOR HE GRANTS SLEEP TO THOSE HE LOVES.

PSALM 127:2

It was the Christmas that Diane's son, Marty, was eight that she witnessed a miracle. Her youngest child, Marty, was filled with an unquenchable spirit even though he had a minor handicap. He was deaf in one ear.

While times had been difficult for her family, Diane knew how much better off she was than Kenny's mom, who lived nearby and struggled daily just to feed and clothe her children.

Several weeks before Christmas, Diane realized that Marty was saving his small allowance for a gift to give to Kenny. One day he strolled into the kitchen and showed her a pocket compass. "I've bought Kenny a present," he said.

Knowing how proud Kenny's mother was, Diane didn't believe she would allow her son to accept a gift if he couldn't give one in return. Marty argued with his mother and finally said, "But what if it was a secret? What if they never found out who gave it?"

Diane finally relented and watched her son walk out the door on Christmas Eve, cross the wet pasture, and slip beneath the electric fence.

~

He raced up to the door and pressed the doorbell, then ran down the steps and across the yard so he wouldn't be seen. Suddenly, the electric fence loomed in front of him, and it smacked him hard. The shock knocked him to the ground, and he gasped for breath. Slowly, he got up and stumbled home.

Diane treated the blister on Marty's face, then put him to bed. The next day, Kenny came to the front door excitedly talking about his new compass. Amazingly, Marty seemed to hear—with both ears.

Later the doctor confirmed that Marty somehow had regained hearing in his deaf ear. Though the doctor said it might have been the shock from the electric fence, Diane believed that miracles still happen on the night we celebrate our Lord's birth.[9]

WHEN YOU GIVE TO THE NEEDY,
DO NOT LET YOUR LEFT HAND
KNOW WHAT YOUR RIGHT HAND
IS DOING, SO THAT YOUR GIVING
MAY BE IN SECRET. THEN YOUR
FATHER, WHO SEES WHAT IS DONE
IN SECRET, WILL REWARD YOU.

MATTHEW 6:3-4

Marine biologists are learning a great deal about the ocean floor these days, thanks to the specially designed one-person submarine. Able to stay submerged for up to eight hours at a time and capable of going as deep as one kilometer, these subs give new meaning to "ocean view"—compliments of a transparent passenger housing made of acrylic. Subs are outfitted with lights, electric thrusters, hydraulic manipulator arms, and scientific, navigational, and life-support equipment.

Despite all the high-tech gadgets, however, this fact remains: It's dark down there! Sunlight travels only so far. After a certain point, some other light source is needed if you're going to observe the wonders of the deep.

The same is true for the deep-sea creatures, many of which emit a form of natural illumination known as bioluminescence. For some, the built-in lighting is used as a defense system. Enemies are sprayed with glowing tissue that turns the hunter into the hunted.

For others, the light provides camouflage. What little sunlight pierces the darkness above them works with the light coming from the creatures' undersides and erases any shadows that might give away their position.[10]

Few of us will ever sink to the level of these creatures, but we understand how they must feel about light. When we're driving on a poorly-lit road late at night, we rely on our cars' headlights to keep us from driving off the pavement. We protect our houses from break-ins by putting floodlights in the yards.

To live in this dark and confusing world, the Lord has put into us His own light, the Holy Spirit. He reveals what is true and good, as well as where we should and should not go. He is our conscience and our guide.

Looking back over your day, can you pinpoint times when the Holy Spirit was giving you direction or indicating what was wrong or right?

═══════

LET YOUR LIGHT SHINE BEFORE MEN, THAT THEY MAY SEE YOUR GOOD DEEDS AND PRAISE YOUR FATHER IN HEAVEN.

MATTHEW 5:16

❧ THE POWER OF PRAYER ❧

Nan stood at the window one winter day watching the wind whipping the pine trees. The cold rain had sneaked in the night before. Early that morning, she had struggled to get out of bed as the extreme cold and dampness wreaked havoc on her joints.

At the post office, everyone seemed to feel as she did. No one smiled, and everyone seemed to be struggling through the day. She decided then and there to at least change her own outlook. She smiled—not a forced smile, but a caring smile that radiated the love of God. For some, she whispered a "flash prayer" that their day would be blessed by the Heavenly Father.

Her smiles brought blessings from God in the form of a grandmother who rushed to her side to share a funny story, a man who asked her opinion on which handbag to buy for his wife, and the boy who allowed her to take his place in the express lane.

Nan remembered how a smile began a friendship with a young grocery store bagger who had Down's syndrome. One winter day, with snow clouds slung low across the sky, the young man carried her groceries to her car. Digging in her purse for a tip,

❧

she was embarrassed when she found she had nothing to give him.

"I'm sorry," she said, not wanting to disappoint the young man.

A smile as bright as the summer sun spread across his face. "That's okay," he said. Then he wrapped his arms around her. "I love you," he said. Shivering in the cold, she whispered a "flash prayer" for this special child of God. "Lord, bless this precious child," she whispered.

Sometimes the most unexpected encounters can teach us a lesson in humility, but the greatest lesson in humility is found in Jesus Christ." Tonight, whisper a "flash prayer" for someone you saw today.

———

DEAR FRIENDS, SINCE GOD SO LOVED US, WE ALSO OUGHT TO LOVE ONE ANOTHER. NO ONE HAS EVER SEEN GOD; BUT IF WE LOVE ONE ANOTHER, GOD LIVES IN US AND HIS LOVE IS MADE COMPLETE IN US.

1 JOHN 4:11-12

❧ RESTORED BY THE MASTER ❧

In a remote Swiss village stood a beautiful church. It was known as the Mountain Valley Cathedral. The church was not only beautiful to look at, with its high pillars and magnificent stained glass windows, but it had the most incredible pipe organ in the entire region. People would come from miles away—even from far-off lands—to hear the lovely tones of this organ.

One day a problem arose. The columns were still there, the windows still dazzled with the sunlight, but an eerie silence enveloped the valley. The area no longer echoed with the glorious fine-tuned music of the pipe organ.

Musicians and experts from around the world tried to repair the instrument. Every time a new person would try to fix it, the villagers were subjected to sounds of disharmony, awful noises that seemed to pollute the air.

One day an old man appeared at the church door. He spoke with the sexton, and after a time the sexton reluctantly agreed to let the old man try his hand at repairing the organ. For two days the old man worked in almost total silence. The sexton was getting a bit nervous.

Then on the third day, at precisely high noon, the valley once again was filled with glorious music.

❧

Farmers dropped their plows; merchants closed their stores; everyone in town stopped what they were doing and headed for the cathedral. Even the bushes and trees of the mountaintops seemed to respond as the glorious music echoed from ridge to ridge.

After the old man finished playing, a brave soul asked him how he could have restored the magnificent instrument when the world's experts could not. The old man merely said, "It was I who built this organ fifty years ago. I created it—and now I have restored it."

God created you, and He knows exactly what you need to live your life to the fullest. As your Creator, He can restore you at the end of a draining day—so you can play beautiful music tomorrow!

THOSE WHO HOPE IN THE LORD WILL RENEW THEIR STRENGTH. THEY WILL SOAR ON WINGS LIKE EAGLES; THEY WILL RUN AND NOT GROW WEARY, THEY WILL WALK AND NOT BE FAINT.

ISAIAH 40:31

❧ HIDDEN TREASURE ❧

Thirty-seven-year-old Joyce Girgenti, a Christian artist, shares her faith by painting the name of Jesus into her inspirational paintings.

One year, Joyce was approached by an organization that wanted her to donate a Christmas card scene. Her first effort, a fireplace scene complete with a Christmas tree and nativity scene, was turned down. Undaunted, Joyce replaced the scene with another, and it was accepted. Later, Joyce realized why her original scene was rejected; God had other plans.

Joyce had used a photo of her own fireplace to paint the original scene. Working from the top of the canvas, she painted the Christmas tree, the nativity on the mantel, the roaring fire, and the stones that formed the fireplace. As she began to paint the bottom of the fireplace, she turned to her daughter. "Wouldn't it be neat to hide something in the fireplace that refers to Christmas?" she asked.

Before her daughter could answer, Joyce said, "What better than Jesus? He's why we celebrate Christmas." She then arranged the fireplace stones to spell out the name of Jesus. At her daughter's urging, she added a stone that resembled a heart.

❧

After her card was rejected, Joyce used it to send to clients and friends. One day, Joyce received a call from her friend, Mary, who asked, "Is Jesus' name really in your fireplace?" She had called to verify what she'd found.

In each of her inspirational paintings, Joyce seeks to please God by painting Jesus' name somewhere in her work. She shares her faith with everyone she meets, saying, "If you forget me, you've lost nothing; but if you forget Jesus, you've lost everything."

It's a mystery trying to find His name so well hidden in Joyce's paintings, but the real mystery is not His name—it's Jesus himself. Only when Jesus is revealed are we able to discern His hidden treasure for us—His gift of salvation.

MY PURPOSE IS THAT THEY MAY BE ENCOURAGED IN HEART AND UNITED IN LOVE, SO THAT THEY MAY HAVE THE FULL RICHES OF COMPLETE UNDERSTANDING, IN ORDER THAT THEY MAY KNOW THE MYSTERY OF GOD, NAMELY, CHRIST, IN WHOM ARE HIDDEN ALL THE TREASURES OF WISDOM AND KNOWLEDGE.

COLOSSIANS 2:2-3

☙ A GOOD NIGHT HUG ❧

For a small child, the most comforting place in the world is in the secure arms of his mother or father. It's not really very different for grown-ups. The embrace of caring arms is a wonderful place to be. Even a brief hug from a casual friend can lift one's spirits.

At the end of a busy or frustrating day, "after the uproar has ceased," grown-ups may long for a pair of loving parental arms to assure them everything's going to be all right—to hear a voice that says soothingly, "I'm here, and I'll take care of you."

Take this little poem as a "hug" tonight from One who loves you without measure, and who watches over your every move with tenderness and compassion:

> When the birds begin to worry
> And the lilies toil and spin,
> And God's creatures all are anxious,
> Then I also may begin.
>
> For my Father sets their table,
> Decks them out in garments fine,
> And if He supplies their living,
> Will he not provide for mine?

☙

Just as noisy, common sparrows
Can be found most anywhere—
Unto some just worthless creatures,
If they perish who would care?

Yet our Heavenly Father numbers
Every creature great and small,
Caring even for the sparrows,
Marking when to earth they fall.

If His children's hairs are numbered,
Why should we be filled with fear?
He has promised all that's needful,
And in trouble to be near.

—Unknown

AFTER THE UPROAR WAS CEASED,
PAUL CALLED UNTO HIM THE
DISCIPLES, AND EMBRACED THEM.

ACTS 20:1 KJV

↜ IN GOD'S HANDS ↜

The last time Allison saw her sister Beth, they had a difference of opinion and decided to go their separate ways. She later learned her sister had turned her back on God.

As the years passed, Allison missed her younger sister and unsuccessfully tried to find her. For a long time, she pleaded with God to help her find Beth. Finally, she stopped begging God to answer her prayers and placed the request in His hands to do what pleased Him. The days, months, and years passed, and it seemed as though her prayers would remain unanswered.

But God had heard her prayers. Two weeks before Christmas in 1998, Allison busied herself decorating the house in the stillness of the late afternoon. As she placed the nativity scene on top of the television set, her thoughts turned to the first Christmas and the Christ child who was God's love gift to the world. How she wished she could share that love with her sister.

Glancing out the window, she saw the mailman stuff another batch of cards into the mailbox.

↜

Wrapping her sweater around her, she went outside. All of the envelopes, except one red one, had return addresses. Curious, she turned it over and opened it.

"Please forgive me, Sis," it read. "I apologize for not getting in touch sooner. I hope we can talk." Allison looked at the enclosed photos, and tears sprang to her eyes. Fifteen years was a long time.

When the sisters finally spoke to each other, Allison was surprised to learn that her once-wayward sister was now a Christian. "I still have the Bible you gave me when I was six," Beth said. "It's still in the original box; and not only that, I use it." To Allison's surprise, God had shared His love gift of Jesus with her sister.

Tonight, put your trust in God and let Him take care of your family.

———

"BE STILL, AND KNOW THAT
I AM GOD; I WILL BE EXALTED
AMONG THE NATIONS, I WILL
BE EXALTED IN THE EARTH."

PSALM 46:10

OUR PROTECTOR AND GUIDE

During World War II, one of the United States' mighty bombers took off from the island of Guam with its deadly cargo. Its target was Kokura, Japan. The sleek B-29 circled for half an hour, then three-quarters of an hour, then fifty-five minutes above the cloud that covered Kokura.

Finally, their gas supply reached the danger point, and they were ordered to fly to a secondary target. It seemed a shame to be right over the primary target and have to pass it up, but there was no choice.

With one more look back, the crew headed for the secondary target, where the sky proved clear. "Bombs away!"—and the B-29 headed for home.

Weeks later, an officer received information from his military intelligence that sent a chill through his heart. Thousands of Allied prisoners of war, the biggest concentration of Americans in enemy hands, had been moved to Kokura a week before the suspended bombing!

"Thank God," breathed the officer. "Thank God for that cloud."

The city which was hidden from the bomber was the site of a massive prison camp, and a simple cloud saved the lives of thousands of Americans. The secondary target that day was Nagasaki. The bomb intended for Kokura was the world's second atomic bomb!

You must make choices every moment of the day. Often those choices affect the lives of others, and at times these decisions are heart-wrenching. In these moments, it is important to remember that you can trust God for His guidance, His wisdom, and His divine protection. Even when we can't see beyond the circumstances and may be afraid to go on, God can see and will lead you in the right path.

THIS GOD IS OUR GOD FOR EVER AND EVER; HE WILL BE OUR GUIDE EVEN TO THE END.

PSALM 48:14

↔ BE A LIGHT ↔

Did you ever go exploring through the woods as a child? Following an unfamiliar path seems like an adventure—until it gets dark. While hiking up a mountainous trail, you lose track of time, and murky shadows creep in. The sound of twigs and leaves cracking under your shoes grows deafening. Your great adventure now turns frightening. Suddenly, you can't see the path in front of you. If only another person would come along with a lantern and lead you back home.

Today, there are many people who walk in darkness. They are confused about their purpose in life and are searching for answers. They need someone to hold out a light and show them the way.

Psalm 18:28 NKJV says, "You will light my lamp; the LORD my God will enlighten my darkness" (NKJV).

In our spiritual darkness of hopelessness and lack of direction, God promises to bring hope to our situation with His brilliant light of wisdom and understanding. Often that wisdom comes through the words of people we know or strangers we meet. Have you walked down a difficult road? Then share what God taught you in that situation. Lead others out of the darkness into a life filled with meaning and purpose. Share God's light with someone who is searching for the truth.

Do you work with young people? Share your experience and wisdom with them. Do you work in a hospital? Treat your patients as you would want to be treated in the same circumstances. Are you lonely and wish you had more friends? Volunteer. Share your God-given gifts and let your heart illuminate the lives of others. By helping other people find meaning for their lives, you'll discover God's purpose for your own.

THEN JESUS SPOKE TO THEM AGAIN, SAYING, "I AM THE LIGHT OF THE WORLD. HE WHO FOLLOWS ME SHALL NOT WALK IN DARKNESS, BUT HAVE THE LIGHT OF LIFE."

JOHN 8:12 NKJV

↬ BEDTIME SONG ↫

The night seems to have different sounds and rhythms than the day. It isn't necessarily that the specific sounds of the night are louder or exclusively belong to the night, although some do. Rather, it is at night that we seem to hear certain sounds more clearly. It is at night that we are likely to notice:

> *The ticking of a clock.*
> *The creak of a stair.*
> *The chirp of a cricket.*
> *The barking of a dog.*
> *The scrape of a twig against the window.*
> *The clatter of a loose shutter.*
>
> *The deep call of a foghorn.*
> *The wind in the trees.*
> *The croaking of a frog.*
> *The opening of a door.*
> *The strains of music down the hall.*
> *The whimper of a child.*
> *The whispers of a spouse.*

It is also at night that we are more prone to listen with our spiritual ears. Frederick Buechner has suggested, "Listen to your life. See it for the fathomless mystery that it is. In the boredom and

pain of it no less than in the excitement and
gladness: touch, taste, smell your way to the holy and
hidden heart of it because in the last analysis all
moments are key moments, and life itself is grace."[12]

> *Listen to the moment.*
> *Listen to your thoughts and feelings.*
> *Listen to your impulses and desires.*
> *Listen to your longings and fears.*
> *Listen to the beat of your own heart.*
> *Listen to God's still small voice in the innermost recesses of*
> *your being.*

Night is for listening. Listen—and learn—with
your spiritual ears, as well as your natural ears.

⸻

I WILL BLESS THE LORD WHO
COUNSELS ME; HE GIVES
ME WISDOM IN THE NIGHT.
HE TELLS ME WHAT TO DO.

PSALM 16:7 TLB

Jeremy's mother heard the front door slam. Her son had ignored her directive to stay home and study for his math test in the morning. Sighing heavily, she wandered into his room, gazing at the gruesome music posters he had hung on his wall. Where was her happy little boy who used to bring her bouquets of wildflowers in a grimy fist? Why had he become so belligerent and rebellious? Where had they gone wrong?

The room held no answers. She and her husband had attended church with him, and Jeremy had always loved Sunday school. But when he turned sixteen, he dropped out of church and started hanging out with guys who dressed in black. Almost overnight, it seemed as if her son had turned into a morose stranger. Weary, Jeremy's mother knelt by his bed and lifted up her heart to God in a three-word prayer, "Help me, Lord!" Prayer was her best defense against the darkness that was stealing her son. A peace settled over her heart.

When teenagers go astray and young adults go against everything that parents have taught them, the parents usually blame themselves. They ask, *Where did I go wrong? What could I have done better? What was the turning point? Should I have reacted differently to their rebellion? Was I too strict in my discipline?*

Even children with the most godly of parents sometimes rebel against God. We teach our children how to choose wisely, but the choices they make are theirs alone, right or wrong, and they bear the responsibility for them.

God has been in the parenting business for a long time. He understands about children going astray and choosing to make the wrong decisions. But God is the God of the second chance! Bring your children before the Lord often and allow Him to keep them in His hands. If they choose to wander off the path, He will know what to do.

HEAR, O HEAVENS, AND GIVE EAR, O EARTH: FOR THE LORD HATH SPOKEN, I HAVE NOURISHED AND BROUGHT UP CHILDREN, AND THEY HAVE REBELLED AGAINST ME.

ISAIAH 1:2 KJV

⚜ OF GREAT VALUE ⚜

"Going . . . going . . . gone!" The bidding was over, and the auctioneer's gavel fell. The winning bid for a rocking chair that had been valued between $3,000 and $5,000 was $453,500.

This had been the case throughout the duration of the auction. A used automobile valued between $18,000 and $22,000 was sold for $79,500. A set of green tumblers valued at $500 sold for $38,000. A necklace valued at $500 to $700 went for $211,500. For four days articles of common, ordinary value were sold for wildly inflated prices. Why? The items auctioned were from the estate of Jacqueline Kennedy Onassis.

How do we assess value? How do we determine what is valuable to us?

As in the sale of the items of the Kennedy estate, some things are valuable solely because of the one to whom they belong. Paul wrote to the Corinthians, "You were bought at a price" (1 Corinthians 6:20 NKJV).

Peter wrote, "You were not redeemed with corruptible things, like silver or gold, . . . but with the precious blood of Christ" (1 Peter 1:18-19 NKJV). The price Paul and Peter are talking about was the price for our sin, paid by Jesus Christ in His death on the cross.

We may inflate a person's worth because of his or her financial status, influence, or potential to benefit us; or we may say a person has no value because he or she has few assets or cannot help us. But the Scriptures tell us that when we were still sinners Jesus Christ died for us. (See Romans 5:8.) When we had no value and were even opposed to God, He paid the price to redeem our lives.

Every individual on the face of the earth is someone for whom Jesus died. Because of the great price of redemption, every single person, regardless of his or her financial worth, is of great importance.

Whenever you feel depressed and worthless, meditate on this: Your value is determined by God. He loved and valued you so much, He sent His Son to die so you could become His child. Never doubt your importance and worth!

YOU ARE CHRIST'S, AND
CHRIST IS GOD'S.

1 CORINTHIANS 3:23 NKJV

Ed Butchart's ministry began in 1981 when he made friends with a man who had cerebral palsy. To his surprise, Butchart found himself helping to change a lightbulb, which was something the man couldn't do himself. It gave Butchart a feeling he'd never experienced—a feeling of sacrificially helping others. From this small beginning, his nonprofit wheelchair ministry started.

Butchart's ministry has grown from a small space in his garage to a 64,500-square-foot warehouse that houses wheelchairs, wheelchair parts, and other similar devices.

In the beginning, Butchart and his wife, Annie, worked tirelessly rebuilding the wheelchairs themselves. Now the ministry boasts a paid staff of eleven, many of whom live with disabilities. Kevin Riggs, the ministry's director of communications and a quadriplegic with cerebral palsy, is responsible for designing the ministry's Web site and writing brochures.

Miracles are a way of life at the ministry. Once a mother and her physically challenged son asked for a 386 personal computer. Before Butchart could explain to them that they didn't have one, a truck unloaded a number of computers. Among them was a working 386 model, which Butchart gave to the family.

~

A few days later, the mother and son came back. "I can't believe this place," the mother said. "You make dreams come true." When the woman hesitated, Butchart asked, "What's your other dream?" The woman asked for a van equipped with a wheelchair lift. But she didn't want just any van; she wanted a Volkswagen van.

Butchart smiled. "Will blue be OK?" In the back of the building stood a blue Volkswagen van, which he repaired before giving it to them.

God has opened countless doors for the ministry, especially during many times when the coffers were empty. After Butchart and his staff pray for finances, God provides what is needed, usually within days. A modest man, Butchart takes no credit but gives all the credit to God.[13]

Tonight, ask God how you can help others.

"IF YOU REMAIN IN ME AND MY
WORDS REMAIN IN YOU, ASK
WHATEVER YOU WISH, AND IT WILL
BE GIVEN YOU. THIS IS TO MY
FATHER'S GLORY, THAT YOU BEAR
MUCH FRUIT, SHOWING YOURSELVES
TO BE MY DISCIPLES."

JOHN 15:7-8

❧ HANDLING THE ❧ SMALL THINGS

A man once said to his new bride, "Honey, I think the best way for our family to operate would be for you to take care of all the small stuff, and let me take care of all the big stuff." His young wife agreed, and so they lived their lives.

At the celebration of their fiftieth wedding anniversary, the couple was asked to share their "secret" to a happy marriage. The husband relayed the agreement they had made as newlyweds. His wife added with a smile, "And I discovered that if I took care of the small stuff, there never was any big stuff to handle!"

Clearing away the small stuff of life—the daily decisions, problem-solving, and nuisances that need to be resolved—can be regarded as a burden, or it can be viewed as paving the way to peace and productivity. It takes just as much effort to remove small stones from a path as it does to arrange them so they make a better path. It's all about your point of view.

This prayer by Mary Stuart reflects a desire to move beyond the small stuff into the truly meaningful:

❧

*Keep me, O Lord, from all pettiness. Let me be large in
  thought and word and deed.*
*Let me leave off self-seeking and have done with
  fault-finding.*
*Help me put away all pretense, that I may meet my neighbors
  face to face, without self-pity and without prejudice.*
*May I never be hasty in my judgments, but generous to all and
  in all things.*
Make me grow calm, serene, and gentle. . . .
*Grant that I may realize that it is the trifling things of life that
  create differences, that in the higher things we are all one.*
And, O Lord, God, let me not forget to be kind![14]

When we handle the small things, we can move
on to the greater things!

THOU HAST BEEN FAITHFUL
OVER A FEW THINGS, I WILL
MAKE THEE RULER OVER MANY
THINGS: ENTER THOU INTO
THE JOY OF THY LORD.

MATTHEW 25:21 KJV

❧ A FORGIVENESS EXCHANGE ❧

It was two weeks before Christmas when Nikki drove toward the mall to exchange Christmas gifts with her friend. A sense of dread hung over her, much like the dark clouds that were threatening rain. A light drizzle began falling, and she switched on the windshield wipers.

For more than eight years, she and Barbara had shared the Christmas holiday at a favorite restaurant, but this year a disagreement had brought on hurt feelings. On the car radio she listened to the songs of the season, but nothing could cheer her up.

Pulling into the parking space, she turned off the engine, wishing she'd never agreed to this lunch. Inside the restaurant, Nikki walked toward a small table near a window. Soon, she saw Barbara drive up, and she steeled herself for a difficult lunch.

"Sorry I'm late," said Barbara, placing a gaily wrapped package on the table.

Both women ordered salads and continued with small talk until they finished their meal. Finally the time came to share their Christmas gifts. Nikki handed Barbara a gift bag while she studied the carefully

❧

wrapped package she was given. Almost in tandem, they opened their gifts. The gifts paled in comparison to what transpired next as the friends were parting.

Nikki picked up her gift, relieved that the awkward occasion was over. Just then, Barbara reached out to her in love, and they exchanged a long, heartfelt embrace. "Thanks so much for the present," Barbara said. "We need to do this again really soon."

As Nikki drove home, she noticed the clouds had lifted and the sun was trying to peek through. She smiled, realizing what she and Barbara had really exchanged was the gift of forgiveness.

Has your heart been mired in hurt, anger, or disappointment? Tonight, allow God to give you a new spirit for forgiving those who have hurt you.

———

THE WAGES OF SIN IS DEATH, BUT
THE GIFT OF GOD IS ETERNAL LIFE
IN CHRIST JESUS OUR LORD.

ROMANS 6:23

❧ NIGHTTIME DEVOTIONS ❧

Bedtime prayers are often limited to reciting a poem or saying a little memorized prayer. However, bedtime prayers can become family devotions if the entire family gathers at the bedside of the child who retires first.

Each member of the family says a heartfelt prayer that is spontaneous and unrehearsed. A verse or two of Scripture might be read prior to prayer. The point of such a devotional time is not that a child is obedient to say a prayer before sleep, but that the child's heart is knit to the heart of God and to the hearts of other family members.

Spontaneous, unrehearsed prayers invite a child to share his or her heart with the Lord. Having each family member pray allows the child to catch a glimpse of their souls and learn from their example how to relate to God, give praise, and make their requests known to a loving Heavenly Father.

Albert Schweitzer once commented on the need for parents to provide an example in devotion:

"From the services in which I joined as a child I have taken with me into life a feeling for what is solemn, and a need for quiet self-recollection, without which I cannot realize the

❧

meaning of my life. I cannot, therefore, support the opinion
of those who would not let children take part in grown-up
people's services till they to some extent understand them.
The important thing is not that they shall understand but
that they shall feel something of what is serious and solemn.
The fact that a child sees his elders full of devotion, and has
to feel something of devotion himself, that is what gives the
service its meaning for him."[15]

End your evening with family devotions. Even if
you don't have children, it's an opportunity to spend
time with your Heavenly Father and sort out the
chaos of the day. He'll help you put everything into
perspective so you can sleep peacefully.

"WHEN YOU PRAY . . . PRAY TO
YOUR FATHER WHO IS IN THE
SECRET PLACE; AND YOUR FATHER
WHO SEES IN SECRET WILL
REWARD YOU OPENLY."

MATTHEW 6:6 NKJV

⤳ A HELPING HAND ⤳

Cathy shares God's comfort with everyone she
meets, especially those who have experienced the ravages
of cancer. She knows much about the disease. Not only
had she undergone surgery for breast cancer in 1990, but
she also had experienced its return—with a vengeance—a
year later. At that point, the only option the doctors gave
her was to have a bone marrow transplant.

After much prayer, Cathy decided in favor of the
transplant, which forced her to stay in isolation for
six weeks in an Atlanta hospital. She was bombarded
with massive doses of chemotherapy twenty-four
hours a day for four days and given blood
transfusions. She was so weak from the assault on her
body that she could barely speak.

Her friends in Christ responded to her need by
offering prayer, encouraging cards, poetry, phone calls,
and food for her family. As a result, Cathy returned
home as an encourager and became an important part
of her cancer support group at the local hospital, where
she spent countless hours helping others.

Once, not long after her bone marrow transplant,
Cathy offered support to a single mother with
recurrent breast cancer. The mother faced a procedure
called stem-cell recovery. Knowing the mother had no

other help, Cathy drove her to the hospital in Atlanta and sat with her through numerous long and painful tests. During one of the tests, as Cathy waited patiently by her bed, the woman embraced her and said, "Thank you so much for all you've done."

Since then Cathy has uplifted and encouraged numerous people facing similar cancer treatments. Cathy has been cancer-free for several years now, and she continues to comfort others as God comforted her in her hour of need.

Cathy acknowledges that God's Spirit used her friends that year to help lift her spirit. Now He works through her life to bless others. Tonight, ask God if there's someone with whom you can share His comfort. Pass it around!

PRAISE BE TO THE GOD AND FATHER OF OUR LORD JESUS CHRIST, THE FATHER OF COMPASSION AND THE GOD OF ALL COMFORT, WHO COMFORTS US IN ALL OUR TROUBLES, SO THAT WE CAN COMFORT THOSE IN ANY TROUBLE WITH THE COMFORT WE OURSELVES HAVE RECEIVED FROM GOD.

2 CORINTHIANS 1:3

❧ ACTS OF KINDNESS ❧

"When I was young I admired clever people. Now that I am old, I admire kind people," said Rabbi Abraham Heschel. From the Jewish perspective, an unkind person does not believe in God.

"How could anyone who believes in the God of the Bible treat his or her fellow human beings, all of whom are created in God's image, with less than compassion?" asks Rabbi Joseph Telushkin.

"Have we not all one Father? Did not one God create us? Why do we profane the covenant of our fathers by breaking faith with one another?" (Malachi 2:10)

The story is told that when Abba Tahnah the Pious was entering his city on the Sabbath eve with a bundle over his shoulder, he came upon a helpless man lying at a crossroads.

The man said to him, "Master, do an act of kindness for me. Carry me into the city."

Abba Tahnah replied, "If I abandon my bundle, how shall I and my household support ourselves? But if I abandon a man afflicted with boils, I will forfeit my life!"

He set down his bundle on the road and carried the afflicted man into the city. Then he returned for his bundle and reentered the city with the last rays of the sun. Everybody was astonished at seeing so pious a man carrying a heavy bundle as the Sabbath was beginning, something forbidden by Jewish law. They exclaimed, "Is this really Abba Tannah the Pious?"

He, too, felt uneasy at heart and said to himself: *Is it possible that I have desecrated the Sabbath?* At that point, the Holy One caused the sun to continue to shine, thereby delaying the beginning of the Sabbath.[16]

> *Each kindly act we do toward men,*
> *Each loving word by voice or pen,*
> *Brings recompense in brotherhood,*
> *And makes the Father understood.*[17]

Pray tonight for opportunities to be kind tomorrow. While it may not be on your "to do" list for the day and may delay a project, your kindnesses toward others count for eternity and show others the nature of your loving Father God.

I WAS EYES TO THE BLIND
AND FEET TO THE LAME.

JOB 29:15

"You might need to come," the nurse said. After receiving calls such as this on many occasions during the last six months, Lorraine was exhausted. Her days were difficult, and her nights were long as she worried about her father. Six months earlier he had been diagnosed with a terminal illness.

The seventy miles to the nursing home was a long trip, especially during desperate times such as this one. On her previous trips, her father was stable by the time she arrived. This time, however, the nurse's voice sounded different. Lorraine's heart was heavy, and her eyes were tired.

While driving, she shouted questions at God. She couldn't understand why God would allow this to happen. She tried to serve Him faithfully, but she felt that God had deserted her and her father.

"Why don't You love me anymore, God?" she cried. Just as the words left her mouth, a bird flew up from the cotton field beside the interstate. It fluttered in front of her windshield and then flew straight up. Her eyes followed it as it flew toward what appeared to be a cross in the sky.

Instantly she realized that God had just answered her plea. *I do love you,* He seemed to say. *I sent My Son to die for you. Remember the Cross!* She began to weep, as she asked for forgiveness for her wavering faith. When she arrived, the nurse met her at the door with good news. Her father's health had once again stabilized.

That event happened almost two years ago, and although her father's health is deteriorating gradually, her faith in God has never faltered again. God told her that He loved her, and that's all she needed to hear.

When her father goes home to be with the Lord, Lorraine is convinced that God will be at her side to hold her up and keep her strong. The promise of the Cross is eternal.

THE MESSAGE OF THE CROSS IS
FOOLISHNESS TO THOSE WHO
ARE PERISHING, BUT TO US
WHO ARE BEING SAVED
IT IS THE POWER OF GOD.

1 CORINTHIANS 1:18

❧ A PEACEFUL RETREAT ❧

Once upon a time, fishing was a survival skill. If
you wanted to eat, you learned how to fish. Much
later it became a form of recreation. In modern
times, it has become a sport, with fishermen
competing to see who can catch the first fish, the
largest fish, the orneriest fish, or the most fish.

For the purist, fishing is still a chance to
commune with nature, to become one with the great
outdoors. Let's face it: The first rule of fishing,
when you're sitting in a boat in the middle of a lake,
is to be quiet! Maybe you can bend this rule in the
ocean, or while standing in a rushing stream with the
water nearly topping your waders, but on a tranquil
lake or pond, quiet is imperative.

For an avid fisherman, fishing does more than
take him away from the noise and confusion of daily
life. By just thinking back to previous fishing trips, he
can momentarily escape his busy day and stuffy office.

He can remember the way the sunlight or
moonlight looked when it hit the water, the sight of
animals or insects going about their business and giving
little or no thought to the human in their midst, the

❧

satisfaction that came from being alone but not lonely, and the times he chose to share his quiet retreats with one or two friends. Memories such as these are like a park bench in a grove of trees on a cool spring day, a place to lie down and take a deep breath.

In this figurative sense, all of us need a boat in the middle of the lake to escape to now and then. We need a place where we can sit down, throw our lines into the water, and wait patiently for the fish to bite. And if they aren't biting—who cares? As any zealous fisherman will tell you, it's not always about filling your bucket. Sometimes it's about enjoying the soft glow of the moonlight, the wind in your face, and the peace that invades your soul.

═══════

WHERE THE RIVER FLOWS
EVERYTHING WILL LIVE.

EZEKIEL 47:9

POLISHING
❧ RELATIONSHIPS ❧

After hours of searching through dusty cartons in
the basement, brushing aside spider webs and dust
bunnies, Kelly found the box that contained the baby
cup that had belonged to her grandmother. It was
wrapped in yellowed newspaper from many years
earlier, as evidenced by the dates on the paper. Kelly
removed the wrapping and discovered that the cup was
now blackened by tarnish. Frustrated and disappointed,
she stuffed the cup back into the carton.

That night Kelly was unable to sleep. After an
hour of tossing and turning, it finally occurred to
her that she was uneasy because her neglect and lack
of concern had allowed the cup to deteriorate. She
got up quickly and retrieved the cup from the
basement. Finding some silver polish, she gently
cleaned the cup until the beautiful silver again was
revealed. With much work and love, she restored the
cup to its original beauty.

Often our relationships with family and friends
tarnish and deteriorate under layers of hurt feelings,
anger, and misunderstanding. Sometimes the
deterioration begins with a comment made in the

❧

heat of the moment, or it may begin under the strain of other stresses. If the air isn't cleared immediately, the relationship tarnishes.

When we put work and love into our relationships, they can be restored. Then we rediscover the beauty that lies underneath the tarnish and realize that it has been there all along.

If you're lying awake tonight, unable to sleep because you've been hurt by a loved one or you've said hurtful words or retaliated in kind, remember the teachings of Jesus and ask forgiveness for yourself and your loved one.[18]

STOP BEING MEAN, BAD-TEMPERED
AND ANGRY. QUARRELING,
HARSH WORDS, AND DISLIKE OF
OTHERS SHOULD HAVE NO PLACE
IN YOUR LIVES. INSTEAD, BE KIND
TO EACH OTHER, TENDERHEARTED,
FORGIVING ONE ANOTHER,
JUST AS GOD HAS FORGIVEN YOU
BECAUSE YOU BELONG TO CHRIST.

EPHESIANS 4:31-32 TLB

❧ A FAMILY DINNER ❧

In our modern society, with frantic schedules, fast-food restaurants, and microwave ovens, family members frequently "catch a meal" whenever and wherever they can, eating it "on the run."

Nevertheless, when we reflect upon the good times we have shared with the family members, our memories often settle upon family meals—not necessarily holiday feasts, but daily family dinner conversation. When we sit at a table with one another, we share not only food, but also we share our lives.

Elton Trueblood has written eloquently about family dinnertime. Perhaps it's time we reinstitute this practice in our lives!

The table is really the family altar! Here those of all ages come together and help to sustain both their physical and their spiritual existence. If a sacrament is "an actual conveyance of spiritual meaning and power by a material process," then a family meal can be a sacrament. It entwines the material and the spiritual in a remarkable way. The food, in and of itself, is purely physical, but it represents human service in its use. Here, at one common table, is the father who has earned, the mother who has prepared or

planned, and the children who share, according to need,
whatever their antecedent participation may have been.

When we realize how a meal shared together can be a spiritual and regenerating experience, we can understand something of why our Lord, when He broke bread with his little company toward the end of their earthly fellowship, told them that as often as they did it, to remember Him. We, too, seek to be members of His sacred fellowship, and irrespective of what we do about the Eucharist, there is no reason why each family meal should not take on something of the character of a time of memory and hope.[19]

When was the last time your family gathered together for a meal?

———————

HE TOOK BREAD, GAVE
THANKS AND BROKE IT,
AND GAVE IT TO THEM.

LUKE 22:19 NKJV

❧ ROCK SOLID ❧

An environmental news network report released in late 1998 indicated that, contrary to what some people believe, the Antarctic ice sheet is not melting rapidly and has been stable for more than a century. The ice sheet is the largest grounded repository of ice on the planet, and some scientists have argued that the melting of this ice sheet would lead to a dramatic rise in sea levels and extensive worldwide flooding.

That news report eased fears for a short while, but then between March 1998 and March 1999, nearly 1,150 square miles of ice shelf collapsed, and another 1,250 square miles of ice shelf disintegrated in January and February 2002.

Scientists continue to argue about the causes and the implications of these events, some noting that the world has had warmer times without human help. Scientific truth shifts with natural events, research, and their theories about what it all means.

God, on the other hand, has been around with the same rock-solid truth for centuries. And that truth will not disintegrate suddenly beneath our feet when things get hot. As our Rock, God will give us the wherewithal to deal with all of our circumstances, no matter how tough they may seem. God and all that He promises will not wear away nor melt. He will calm our fears and ease our trepidation with the same truth about himself that He used centuries ago with Abraham, David, and Isaiah.

Your life may be unsettled and stormy, causing you to feel as if you were bouncing about on rough waters. But if you allow God to enter into your life, He will melt away your fears and concerns and bring a spring-like freshness to your heart.

As you meditate tonight in preparation for sleep, let God help you prepare for tomorrow. Pray to Him for guidance in your daily decisions. Let Him be your guiding hand in all you do. Let Him rock you gently to sleep, and trust Him to bring you through the rough waters tomorrow. Let Him be your rock and your refuge.[20]

HE ALONE IS MY ROCK AND MY SALVATION; HE IS MY FORTRESS, I WILL NOT BE SHAKEN. MY SALVATION AND MY HONOR DEPEND ON GOD; HE IS MY MIGHTY ROCK, MY REFUGE.

PSALM 62:6-7

᚛ WHAT IS A HOME? ᚛

Ernestine Schuman-Heink is not the first to ask, "What is a home?" But her answer is one of the most beautiful ever penned:

A roof to keep out the rain. Four walls to keep out the wind. Floors to keep out the cold. Yes, but home is more than that. It is the laugh of a baby, the song of a mother, the strength of a father. Warmth of loving hearts, light from happy eyes, kindness, loyalty, comradeship. Home is first school and first church for young ones, where they learn what is right, what is good and what is kind. Where they go for comfort when they are hurt or sick. Where fathers and mothers are respected and loved. Where children are wanted. Where the simplest food is good enough for kings because it is earned. Where money is not so important as lovingkindness. Where even the tea-kettle sings from happiness. That is a home. God bless it. [21]

God asks us to call Him "Father," and family life is at the heart of the Gospel. Through Jesus Christ, God the Father has forged a way to adopt many children. As a result, the Scriptures have much to say about what a happy home should be like. Good family life is never an accident, but an achievement by those who share it.

᚛

When our Heavenly Father is the center of our homes, our homes will be a reflection of Him. But sometimes this is easier said than done. That's why He gives us sixty-six books of the Bible to help us! We must learn His way of thinking and doing things. Then we must teach our children what He teaches us.

Keeping the home fires burning is letting God's Word and presence guide your way and keeping the love of God ablaze in the hearts of your family.

———

TEACH THE YOUNG WOMEN TO BE SOBER, TO LOVE THEIR HUSBANDS, TO LOVE THEIR CHILDREN.

TITUS 2:4 KJV

❧ WORKING AT NIGHT ❧

Ah, the moon is up. Doesn't that make you feel like getting up, eating breakfast, and going off to work?

No? Then you're like most people who naturally want to sleep at night and work and play during the daylight hours. But for some, their jobs require them to march to a different beat—to sleep during the day and be alert, active, and productive at night. While the world sleeps around them, many are up working the night shift.

If you are among those who must work late at night, life may seem lonely. Your clock is set for an evening wake-up call, while others' are set for the morning. If a friend suggests playing tennis at noon, you know you'd feel more like it in the middle of the night, but you'd have a tough time finding a willing friend and a court lit up in the wee hours of the morning.

At times, it may seem as if a friend is nowhere to be found. You are not alone though. God is a friend who is always there for you. No matter whether it is day or night, you can spend time with God because He never slumbers nor sleeps.

❧

During the dark nighttime experiences of life, it may not be easy to praise God. But it's during these dark seasons that God puts a song in your heart. Psalm 77:6 KJV reads: "I call to remembrance my song in the night." God replaces your discouragement with a song.

While imprisoned in Philippi, Paul and Silas were able to lift up their hands and voices in praise to God after being beaten and placed in stocks. They were on the night shift, and God heard their prayers and praise and sent deliverance. You, too, are serving God on the night shift. He will hear and answer your prayers as well.

BEHOLD, BLESS YE THE LORD,
ALL YE SERVANTS OF THE LORD,
WHICH BY NIGHT STAND IN
THE HOUSE OF THE LORD.

PSALM 134:1 KJV

❧ SLEEP DEPRIVED ❧

How can young doctors be on duty nearly twenty-four hours at a time, day after day, and still be alert in a crisis?

Belgian researchers decided to do a study of hospital residents and the effects of their grueling schedules. Stress levels were measured after residents worked a twenty-four-hour shift that encompassed the emergency room, regular ward duties, and the intensive-care unit, followed by a return to the ward at the end of the shift.

Although lack of sleep played a part in raising levels of stress-related hormones, the researchers concluded that a heavy workload on top of important responsibilities was the foremost factor in creating stress. Another way of looking at the research is to say, it's still possible to do an excellent job, even when you're exhausted.

Have you ever tried to stay up for more than twenty-four hours? It's a near-impossible feat for most of us. Some scientists believe that sleep-inducing chemicals build up in the brain and eventually knock us out. But with certain jobs (such as being a

❧

physician) or round-the-clock responsibilities (such as parenting), some of us are occasionally called upon to pull double duty.

Rested or not, we have to be ready to jump into action at a moment's notice. We can do it—especially if we've managed to keep our normal workload and responsibilities within bounds.

In a medical emergency, it takes several people to perform all the ministrations required, and it requires shift work to be sure everyone is rested enough to do their jobs well.[22]

In your times of need, be willing to ask others for help. And above all, seek the help of your Heavenly Father, who never sleeps. He is able to watch over you and provide for you every waking—and sleeping—moment.

———

HE WHO KEEPS YOU WILL
NOT SLUMBER. BEHOLD,
HE WHO KEEPS ISRAEL SHALL
NEITHER SLUMBER NOR SLEEP.

PSALM 121:3-4 NKJV

Jennifer was resting after returning home from a weekend retreat with her husband when she heard the door open.

"Hello!" a familiar voice said. "Anybody home?"

Both Jennifer and Kevin hurried to the door to greet their daughter. At twenty years of age, Becky was trying to discover her place in the world. Gradually, she was attempting to let go of her parents and enter a world of new beginnings.

Letting go of their children had been difficult for the couple. Since Becky was the baby of the family and the only girl, it was even more difficult. Jennifer had spent many sleepless nights worrying about her daughter. At night when Jennifer would hear the door unlock, signaling Becky's safe return, she would whisper a prayer of thanks to God for placing His protective hand over her.

As the nights passed, she learned to depend on God more and more. She realized that even though she couldn't be with Becky every moment of every day, God could. Over the previous year, she had placed her daughter in the hands of God, allowing

Him to guide her steps. This made the nights a lot less worry-filled.

"I'm glad you're home," Becky said as she hugged and kissed her mom and dad. "I missed you both so much." They had been away for only two nights, but to Becky it seemed like an eternity. While she wasn't home much herself, she wanted her parents to be nearby just in case she needed them.

Aren't we glad that God is always home? He never leaves our side and always offers the security that we need to live each day to its fullest. Through the darkness of the night and the brilliance of the day, He remains faithful and true. Thank You, God, for living with us in our home, the greatest earthly gift ever given.

THE LORD'S CURSE IS ON
THE HOUSE OF THE WICKED,
BUT HE BLESSES THE HOME
OF THE RIGHTEOUS.

PROVERBS 3:33

❧ GENTLENESS ❧

"Gentleness" is a soothing, comforting word. It evokes thoughts of peace and rest. We long for a sense of this peace in our homes. We desire an uninterrupted time of relaxation before we retire—bedtime beverages and conversations that are soothing and edifying, a night free of terrors, and dreams that are beautiful. We desire to be treated gently. Gentleness marks an environment we find comforting, uplifting, and calming.

Garrison Keillor described a gentle life in this way:

> *"What keeps our faith cheerful is the extreme persistence of gentleness and humor. Gentleness is everywhere in daily life, a sign that faith rules through ordinary things: through cooking and small talk, through storytelling, making love, fishing, tending animals and sweet corn and flowers, through sports, music, and books, raising kids—all the places where the gravy soaks in and grace shines through. Even in a time of elephantine vanity and greed, one never has to look far to see the campfires of gentle people. Lacking any other purpose in life, it would be good enough to live for their sake."* [23]

While gentleness is a quality of environment we desire, we must recognize that gentleness begins within the heart. Gentleness is described in the

Scriptures as one of the "fruits of the Spirit" (Galatians 5:22-23).

Choose to deal with your family members and friends with gentleness this evening—with kindness, simplicity, and tenderness. In planting seeds of gentleness, you will reap a gentle evening in which to relax and find rest for your body, mind, and soul.

———————

HE WILL FEED HIS FLOCK LIKE A SHEPHERD; HE WILL GATHER THE LAMBS WITH HIS ARM, AND CARRY THEM IN HIS BOSOM, AND GENTLY LEAD THOSE WHO ARE WITH YOUNG.

ISAIAH 40:11 NKJV

↠ RICH IN LOVE ↞

Amy, a young mother, longed to be rich, thinking that wealth would ease the financial strain on her self-employed husband. They lived in a moderate middle-class home, but Amy wanted a more expensive one.

One day Amy visited her sister, Janice, in her new home, and she was impressed. A chandelier hung from the dining room ceiling. The kitchen featured every built-in appliance and gadget possible. The den boasted a large-screen television, loads of CDs, and an enviable stereo system.

Amy thought, *Joe and I could enjoy a home like this, too, if I went to work.*

Later, after the tour of the house was over, Amy asked her sister what time she had to get up for work every morning.

"Five-thirty," Janice said.

Back in her own home, Amy looked at her husband with tears of gratitude in her large brown eyes.

"Do you realize how rich we are?" she asked Joe.

"What do you mean?" Joe frowned.

"I don't have to get up early in the morning and leave our precious son at a sitter's house. I can enjoy him all day. I'm rich! I just never realized it before."

↠↞

Joe laughed, grabbed Amy, hugged her and said, "I totally agree."

In our society, it's so easy to get caught up in material things. Everywhere we look, advertisements appear before us, enticing us to buy a beautiful home, luxurious furniture, designer clothes, late-model cars, boats, motorcycles, and cosmetics.

Tonight, take a look at your surroundings. Notice how rich you are—maybe not with expensive, material objects, but with the things that count. Do you have a pile of library books on your sofa? Or nutritious foods in the cupboard? Or maybe on your refrigerator you have a priceless photo of your child.

No matter what you own, take note of your blessings tonight and enjoy them.

———

THE SLEEP OF A LABORER IS SWEET,
WHETHER HE EATS LITTLE OR
MUCH, BUT THE ABUNDANCE OF A
RICH MAN PERMITS HIM NO SLEEP.

ECCLESIASTES 5:12

Eternity is a difficult concept for us to grasp. In human terms, it seems a matter of time—or more accurately, timelessness. But eternity is more than a measure of time. Things said to be "eternal" have a quality of permanence. The benefits of eternal things are not found solely in the hereafter; they provide an incredible sense of satisfaction in this life as well.

The late Lorado Taft, one of America's great artists, often said that a real work of art must have in it "a hint of eternity." The writer of Ecclesiastes says that God has not only made everything beautiful, but He has set eternity in the heart of man. (See Ecclesiastes 3:11.) When we do a good piece of work, whether it is part of our vocation or not, we may find in it a hint of eternity, the abiding value that outlasts silver or gold.

Daniel Webster, one of America's most famous statesmen, once said: "If we work on marble, it will perish; if on brass, time will efface it; if we rear temples, they will crumble into dust; but if we work on immortal souls and imbue them with principles, with the just fear of God and love of our fellowmen, we engrave on those tablets something that will brighten to all eternity."

Ascending to the top of one of the magnificent stairways in the Library of Congress, one reads this inscription on the wall: "Too low they build who build beneath the stars."

In building your life, build with God for eternity. In building the church, build to the glory of Jesus Christ for the salvation of souls.

Ask the Lord to show you tonight how to make your life and effort count for eternity. Pray for an awareness of eternity as you face every decision and task tomorrow.

WE FIX OUR EYES NOT ON WHAT IS SEEN, BUT ON WHAT IS UNSEEN. FOR WHAT IS SEEN IS TEMPORARY, BUT WHAT IS UNSEEN IS ETERNAL.

2 CORINTHIANS 4:18

↢ STAY AWAKE ↣

"Why aren't you asleep?" a prison inmate yelled
at a guard who was being held hostage during a riot
at a maximum-security prison. "It's the middle of
the night!"

At age sixty-three, the guard, Alex, was the
oldest hostage. Even though he had fought in three
wars and had been trained for combat, he was scared.

"I'm not sleeping because I've been taught that
sometimes it's necessary not to sleep at night but to
stay awake," Alex told the inmate. "I figured tonight
was such a situation. I'm looking out for my safety. I
want to be able to defend myself if an inmate bursts
in here and tries to kill me."

Then a strange thing happened. The inmate
studied Alex for a moment and said, "You're a smart
man." Instead of attacking Alex with the homemade
knife he held, the inmate left the guard in the cell.

Alex watched other inmates run back and forth.
His heart pounded. He didn't know from one
moment to the next what was going to happen. He
thought of his family and friends. He had no idea if
he'd see them again. Unlike some of the other

↣

1 0 4

hostages, Alex escaped the situation without injuries even though about sixty inmates were armed with homemade knives during the two-day riot.

Sometimes we have to be awake at night even if we'd prefer to be sleeping. Maybe you're one of those people. Your situation probably isn't as dramatic as that of the prison guard. But whatever the reason you are up tonight, find satisfaction and peace in the knowledge that eventually you will be able to sleep and get the rest your body requires. Sometimes it's necessary not to sleep at night but to stay awake, being ever vigilant in the task God has set before you.

———

UNDERSTAND THIS: IF THE OWNER OF THE HOUSE HAD KNOWN AT WHAT TIME OF NIGHT THE THIEF WAS COMING, HE WOULD HAVE KEPT WATCH AND WOULD NOT HAVE LET HIS HOUSE BE BROKEN INTO.

MATTHEW 24:43

❧ CHILDLIKE FAITH ❧

Many a parent has stood in awe by the bed of
their sleeping child, amazed at the miracle of his life,
captured by his sweet expression of innocence, and
bewildered by his ability to sleep peacefully regardless
of the turmoil that may be around him.

Those same parents have also felt great
frustration earlier in the day when the child was
willful or disobedient, and they marveled at their
child's ingenuity, energy, curiosity, or humor.
Children seem to embody all of life's extremes.

What did Jesus mean when He said we must receive
and welcome the kingdom of God as a little child?
Surely He meant we must accept and embrace God's
will for our lives with a sense that "this is what is, and
isn't it grand"—welcoming the Lord's will without
debate, without question, without worry or fear, and
with a sense of delight, expectation, and eagerness.

As a child opens a present, he has no doubt that
the pretty paper and ribbon hide a happy surprise. In
the same way, we must anticipate that the kingdom of
God is a joyful and wonderful gift to us, one in
which we can delight thoroughly.

❧

Andrew Gillies has written a lovely poem to describe the childlikeness the Lord desires to see in us. Let it inspire your own prayer tonight:

> Last night my little boy confessed to me
> Some childish wrong;
> And kneeling at my knee,
> He prayed with tears—
> "Dear God, make me a man like Daddy—
> Wise and strong; I know you can!"
>
> Then while he slept I knelt beside his bed,
> Confessed my sins,
> And prayed with low-bowed head—
> "O God, make me a child like my child here—
> Pure, guileless,
> Trusting Thee with faith sincere."[24]

TRULY I TELL YOU, WHOEVER DOES NOT RECEIVE AND ACCEPT AND WELCOME THE KINGDOM OF GOD LIKE A LITTLE CHILD [DOES] POSITIVELY SHALL NOT ENTER IT AT ALL.

MARK 10:15 AMP

⤳ HE MAKES ME LIE DOWN ⤳

One night Mary Lu's eight-month-old baby cried every few minutes. Exhausted from the daytime chores of motherhood, she didn't want to slip out of her warm bed again, but she knew she had to make her baby comfortable for the night.

She plopped her feet on the cold floor and dashed to the nursery. In the glow of the dim night-light, the first thing Mary Lu noticed was that Brad's diaper, gown, and T-shirt were soaked. She took off his clothes, washed him with warm water, dried his soft body with a fluffy towel, and sprinkled baby powder on him.

As she tended to Brad's needs, he kept fussing. When Mary Lu tried to put a dry diaper on him, he kicked it off. Finally she managed to fasten the diaper before he could kick it off again and slipped a clean nightgown on him. Still the baby fussed.

"Shh," Mary Lu shushed, gently encouraging her baby to stop crying. *If only Brad could understand that in just a few minutes he'll be able to go back to sleep!* she thought in exasperation.

Finally, as Mary Lu rubbed his back and sang softly to him, Brad drifted off to sleep. Soon he was snoring softly.

On her way back to bed, Mary Lu suddenly thought of a Bible verse she'd never understood as a child: "He makes me lie down in green pastures . . ." (Psalm 23:2 NRSV).

She realized that although Brad didn't understand it, God used her to provide "green pasture" for him. She thought of the times when she fussed at God in the same way that Brad did at her, until later, when she realized God was actually blessing her and making her to lie down in green pastures.

Remember to rest and treat yourself to green pastures tomorrow. Take a walk in the park, read a good book, or visit a close friend.

HE MAKES ME LIE DOWN IN
GREEN PASTURES; HE LEADS
ME BESIDE STILL WATERS;
HE RESTORES MY SOUL.

PSALM 23:2-3 NRSV

THE GLORY
⊶ OF TOMORROW ⊷

The ability to see "beyond the sunset"—to anticipate the glories of God's tomorrow—enables a Christian to live joyfully and victoriously in any of life's circumstances.

Virgil P. Brock tells how he wrote the beloved hymn "Beyond the Sunset":

> "This song was born during a conversation at the dinner table, one evening in 1936, after watching a very unusual sunset at Winona Lake, Indiana, with a blind guest, my cousin Horace Burr, and his wife, Grace. A large area of the water appeared ablaze with the glory of God, yet there were threatening storm clouds gathering overhead. Our blind guest excitedly remarked that he had never seen a more beautiful sunset.
>
> "'People are always amazed when you talk about seeing,' I told him. 'I can see,' Horace replied. 'I see through other people's eyes, and I often see more; I see beyond the sunset.'
>
> "The phrase 'beyond the sunset' and the striking inflection of his voice struck me so forcibly, I began singing the first few measures. 'That's beautiful!' his wife interrupted. 'Please go to the piano and sing it.'
>
> "We went to the piano nearby and completed the first verse. Before the evening meal was finished, all four stanzas had been written, and we sang the entire song together."

⊶

The first verse of his beautiful hymn says:

Beyond the sunset, O blissful morning,
when with our Savior heav'n is begun.
Earth's toiling ended, O glorious dawning—
beyond the sunset when day is done. [25]

———

NOW WE SEE BUT A POOR
REFLECTION AS IN A MIRROR;
THEN WE SHALL SEE FACE TO
FACE. NOW I KNOW IN PART;
THEN I SHALL KNOW FULLY,
EVEN AS I AM FULLY KNOWN.

1 CORINTHIANS 13:12

❧ NIGHTTIME VISITOR ❧

The hospital room was quiet. Natalie, who was new to the area, was facing an emergency operation in the morning. Knowing only a few people in this small town added to her fear. She was alone in the hospital room, unable to sleep, and as the night dragged along she became more and more nervous. The quietness of the room closed in on her.

She was ready to cry when she heard the creaking of the door. She looked toward it and saw a kind young face.

"Hi," the young woman said. "Are you lonely?"

"I sure am," Natalie replied.

"I'm a nursing student and have been observing here for a couple of weeks. I've caught up on all my paperwork. Do you feel like talking?" she asked.

"I sure do," Natalie replied gratefully. She straightened her pillow and slowly propped herself up in bed.

The compassion in the student's eyes comforted Natalie as their conversation soon turned to God and His wonderful and amazing grace. During the conversation, the heavy burden of fear in Natalie's heart began to lift. After a couple of hours, she

❧

finally drifted off to sleep. The young woman quietly left the room.

Natalie never saw the student nurse again. She couldn't even remember her name. But she never forgot the comfort and peace that settled over her as the young woman shared her love of Jesus Christ. The next morning, Natalie asked about the student nurse, but no one on the new shift had a clue as to her identity.

What had started out as one of the darkest nights of her life had ended in peaceful contentment and sweet dreams, thanks to a young student with a kind heart. Whether the young woman was a celestial angel or an earthly angel of mercy, she was an angel indeed. She brought peace to Natalie's heart and joy to her soul. Isn't that precisely what God sends His angels to do?

DO NOT FORGET TO ENTERTAIN STRANGERS, FOR BY SO DOING SOME PEOPLE HAVE ENTERTAINED ANGELS WITHOUT KNOWING IT.

HEBREWS 13:2

∼ UNCHANGING LOVE ∼

A Scottish minister, George Matheson, who was totally blind, penned the beautiful hymn, "O Love That Will Not Let Me Go." While he would never disclose what triggered the beautiful lyrics, it was widely speculated that his sister's wedding reminded him of a heartbreaking event. Just before he was to wed his college sweetheart, she was told of his impending blindness. She is said to have informed him, "I do not wish to be the wife of a blind preacher." Matheson gives this account:

> "My hymn was composed . . . the night of my sister's marriage. . . . Something happened to me, which was known only to myself, and which caused me the most severe mental suffering. The hymn was the fruit of that suffering. It was the quickest bit of work I ever did in my life. I had the impression of having it dictated to me by some inward voice rather than of working it out myself."

Having experienced rejection from an earthly lover, Matheson wrote of a heavenly Lover whose love is eternal and faithful:

> O Love that wilt not let me go,
> I rest my weary soul on Thee;

I give Thee back the life I owe,
that in Thine ocean depths its flow
may richer, fuller be.

O Light that follow'st all my way,
I yield my flick'ring torch to Thee;
my heart restores its borrowed ray,
that in Thy sunshine's blaze its day
may brighter, fairer be.[26]

The love that first drew you to God is the same love that now surrounds you tonight and will be with you forever, in all situations. Whatever you are going through, allow Him to comfort you.

═══════

"I HAVE LOVED YOU WITH AN EVERLASTING LOVE; I HAVE DRAWN YOU WITH LOVING-KINDNESS."

JEREMIAH 31:3

❧ NO PLACE LIKE HOME ❧

Throughout his life, Glen worked hard. In addition to his regular full-time job, he worked as an automobile mechanic. It didn't matter what hour of the day or night his customers needed his help, he was always ready to come to their rescue. Diligently, he worked to get their cars running again.

He looked forward with eagerness to his retirement. He wanted to travel around the country and show his wife all the things that she had only dreamed of seeing. While he used the money that he earned at his full-time job for bills and living expenses, he saved every dime he made repairing cars. He called that his honeymoon account. He had never taken his wife on a formal honeymoon, and he intended to begin their trip right after he retired. He was so proud of himself for planning their vacation of a lifetime.

When Glen realized how much he had saved, he was amazed. He had enough money to buy a recreational vehicle, with money to spare. After he made the purchase, he and his wife left for their long-awaited honeymoon. They were gone for only a few days when, to everyone's surprise, they returned home.

"There's just no bed like ours," Glen said when others asked why he was back so soon. "When the sun went down, we both missed home so much." With a twinkle in his eye he said, "Home is where the heart is, and my heart is here, especially at night."

Before long, Glen could be seen in the wee hours of the morning laboring over yet another car. With a renewed smile on his face, he sold the recreational vehicle and made a promise to his wife. "Until God calls us to our home in the sky, we'll never leave this place again, honey. There's simply no place like home."

===

"IF ANYONE LOVES ME,
HE WILL OBEY MY TEACHING.
MY FATHER WILL LOVE HIM,
AND WE WILL COME TO HIM AND
MAKE OUR HOME WITH HIM."

JOHN 14:23

~ PICTURE PERFECT ~

When we come to the end of the day and wonder why things went wrong, we usually don't have to look very far to discover the answer. Somehow, we lost our sense of direction and couldn't seem to get back on track. To ensure this doesn't happen again, or at least not as often, we can take some advice from National Geographic photographer Dewitt Jones.

1. Before he goes out to a shoot, Jones knows he has to have a good camera with the right lens. Different lenses give different perspectives. Jones experiments until he finds the right one. If there's a problem at work that has you stymied, try looking at it from different points of view. Pray for "the eyes of your understanding to be enlightened." (See Ephesians 1:18.)

2. Another important factor is focus. With a turn of the lens, the whole picture can be razor sharp, or if Jones prefers, just the subject in the foreground will be clearly in focus. We sometimes become so focused on one aspect of a problem that we lose sight of the big picture—of other circumstances influencing the situation or how the problem is going to affect others if it isn't resolved properly. Look

at the big picture, and then consider all individuals involved.

3. Jones allows his creative instincts to drive him to find more than one "right" way to shoot a photo. He uses about four hundred rolls of film per article—and each published article uses approximately fifty photos. Don't be afraid of experimenting with new ideas and methods. Ask God to show you "great and mighty things that you haven't known before." (See Jeremiah 33:3.) When Dewitt Jones empties his camera at the end of a shoot, he knows he's given it his best shot. He's looked at the subject he's photographing in as many different ways as he can think of.[27]

If we've found the right perspective, stayed focused on what's truly important, been willing to try something different, and refused to let fear of failure paralyze us, we too can look back at our day and say, "Print it!"

BE VERY CAREFUL, THEN,
HOW YOU LIVE—NOT AS
UNWISE BUT AS WISE, MAKING
THE MOST OF EVERY OPPORTUNITY.

EPHESIANS 5:15-16

☙ DAY OF REST ☙

Some years ago, a research physician made an extensive study of the amount of oxygen a person needs throughout the day. He was able to demonstrate that the average workman breathes thirty ounces of oxygen during a day's work, but he uses thirty-one. At the close of the day, he is one ounce short, and his body is tired.

He goes to sleep and breathes more oxygen than he uses to sleep, so in the morning he has regained five-sixths of the ounce he was short. The night's rest does not fully balance the day's work!

By the seventh day, he is six-sixths or one whole ounce in debt again. He must rest an entire day to replenish his body's oxygen requirements.

Further, he demonstrated that replenishing an entire ounce of oxygen requires thirty to thirty-six hours (one 24-hour day plus the preceding and following nights) when part of the resting is done while one is awake and moving about.

Over time, failure to replenish the oxygen supply results in the actual death of cells and, eventually, the premature death of the person.

☙

A person is restored as long as he or she takes the seventh day as a day of rest.[28]

Sound familiar? The God who created us not only invites us to rest. He created our bodies in such a fashion that they demand rest.

Most people think that "keeping the Sabbath" is solely an act of devotion to God. But in turning your attention to Him, He can offer you true rest and replenishment in every area of your life—spirit, soul, and body. He is not only our daily strength; He is our source of rest, recreation, and replenishment.

———

THERE REMAINS, THEN, A SABBATH-REST FOR THE PEOPLE OF GOD; FOR ANYONE WHO ENTERS GOD'S REST ALSO RESTS FROM HIS OWN WORK, JUST AS GOD DID FROM HIS.

HEBREWS 4:9-10

⌁ PRIORITIES ⌁

Jenny Lind, known as "The Swedish Nightingale," won worldwide success as a talented opera singer. She sang for heads of state in many nations and thrilled hundreds of thousands of people in an era when all performances were live.

Not only did her fame grow, but her fortune increased as well. Yet at the height of her career, at a time when her voice was at its peak, she left the stage and never returned.

She must have missed the fame, the money, and the applause of thousands—or so her fans surmised—but Jenny Lind was content to live in quiet seclusion with her husband.

Once an English friend went to visit her. He found her on the beach with a Bible on her knee. As he approached, he saw that her attention was fixed upon a magnificent sunset.

They talked of the old days and former acquaintances, and eventually the conversation turned to her new life. "How is it that you came to abandon the stage at the apex of your career?"

Jenny offered a quiet answer that reflected her peace of heart: "When every day it made me think less of this (laying a finger on the Bible) and nothing at all of that (pointing to the sunset), what else could I do?"

Has a busy, successful life robbed you of some of the most precious gifts of God? Next time you miss a sunset or prayer time because of a crowded schedule, remember Jenny's priorities.

Nothing in life is as precious as your relationship with your Heavenly Father, and then your relationships with family members and friends. Ultimate fulfillment comes not in career or money, but in relationship with God and others.

IF SERVING THE LORD SEEMS
UNDESIRABLE TO YOU, THEN
CHOOSE FOR YOURSELVES THIS
DAY WHOM YOU WILL SERVE . . . .
BUT AS FOR ME AND MY HOUSEHOLD,
WE WILL SERVE THE LORD.

JOSHUA 24:15

↜ N I G H T L Y R E V I E W ↜

In *You Don't Have to Be Blind to See,* Jim Stovall writes:

"Your values determine your character, and
they set a framework for the choices you make
as well as a framework for evaluating your
success. In other words, your values provide
the framework for self-accountability. . . .

"Each night before I go to bed, I review the day
I've just lived. And I evaluate it. I say about
various things I've done or said, and about the
choices I've made, 'That was good. That was
great. That wasn't so hot.' In appraising my
actions and decisions, I'm able to make
midcourse corrections as I pursue my goals. In
appraising my deeds of a day, I can close my
eyes and have a sense of accomplishment, of
being one step closer to the fulfillment of my
destiny on earth."[29]

Reviewing the day and your values against the
criteria of God's Word is a valuable exercise. It allows
you to eliminate regret and pride, and you can wipe
the slate clean for tomorrow's divine handwriting.

When you recall things about which you have
remorse or sorrow, ask the Lord to forgive you for
your sin, give you strength to turn from it,

compensate for your errors, and help you to make amends wherever possible.

When you recall things about which you are pleased, give praise to the Lord for the wisdom, strength, and ability He provided throughout the day. Ask Him to use your "good deeds" and "right judgments" to expand His kingdom on the earth.

Before bed, put both good and bad in God's hands. You can rest in hope for tomorrow, because His mercy and compassion give you a new opportunity to set things right, build on the good, and move forward in His power and love.

THIS I RECALL TO MY MIND,
THEREFORE HAVE I HOPE. IT IS
OF THE LORD'S MERCIES THAT
WE ARE NOT CONSUMED, BECAUSE
HIS COMPASSIONS FAIL NOT.

LAMENTATIONS 3:21-22 KJV

❧ TRUE HUMILITY ❧

If asked whether it's better to be proud or humble, most people would say "humble," since we have been taught that pride is a sin. However, if we think being humble means we are to denigrate ourselves or settle for mediocrity, we have the wrong definition of humility.

Humility is remaining teachable in all situations, knowing God is so much greater and we have so much to learn. Humility comes when we recognize that God loves us just the way we are, that He will be patient as we strive to become like Him in character and word and deed.

Motivational speaker and author Denis Waitley has written:

> "When you come down to the bottom line, joy is accepting yourself as you are right now—an imperfect, changing, growing, and worthwhile person. Realize that liking yourself and feeling that you're an OK individual in your own special way is not necessarily egotistical. Take pride in what you are accomplishing, and even more importantly, enjoy the unique person you are just in being alive right now.

❧

Understand the truth that although we as individuals are not born with equal physical and mental attributes, we are born with equal rights to feel the excitement and joy in believing we deserve the very best in life."[30]

If you scored a victory today, if you won the prize, if you did the right thing, if you moved beyond yourself and extended an act of love and charity to another human being, rejoice in it! Delight in your awareness that the Lord is working in your life and through your life.

To delight in the Lord's work isn't pride. It's a form of praise to your Father, who is proud of you and also proud any time you succeed according to His principles and design. All the glory goes to Him. It is because of Him that we can succeed.

IN HIM WE LIVE AND MOVE
AND HAVE OUR BEING.

ACTS 17:28

❧ BEAUTY IN THE ❧ SUNSET YEARS

Helen Keller was once asked how she would approach old age. She responded:

"Age seems to be only another physical handicap, and it excites no dread in me. Once I had a dear friend of eighty, who impressed upon me the fact that he enjoyed life more than he had done at twenty-five. 'Never count how many years you have, as the French say,' he would insist, 'but how many interests you have. Do not stale your days by taking for granted the people about you, or the things which make up your environment, and you will ever abide in a realm of fadeless beauty.'

"It is as natural for me, certainly, to believe the richest harvest of happiness comes with age as that true sight and hearing are within, not without. Confidently I climb the broad stairway that love and faith have built to heights where I shall 'attain to a boundless reach of sky.'"[31]

The poem "How Old Are You?" reinforces this idea that outlook is what determines our age:

Age is a quality of mind:
If you have left your dream behind,
If hope is cold,
If you no longer look ahead,
If your ambition fires are dead—
Then you are old.
But if from life you take the best,
And if in life you keep the jest,
If love you hold;
No matter how the years go by,
No matter how the birthdays fly,
You are not old.[32]

Years before we reach what we would call "old age," we determine whether that time will be a gracious and pleasant time or a time when we rehearse life's hurts with bitterness. The attitudes with which we invest our days now will characterize the days of our senior years.

———

THE RIGHTEOUS FLOURISH LIKE
THE PALM TREE. . . . THEY STILL
BRING FORTH FRUIT IN OLD AGE.

PSALM 92:12,14 RSV

✿ UNDER CONTROL ✿

It's virtually impossible for you to sleep if you are "wound up." Do memories of the day's events keep you from falling asleep? Do you sometimes feel as if you spent the day pushing a boulder up a mountain with a very small stick? Memorize these words:

> *I lift up my eyes to the hills—where does my help come from? My help comes from the LORD, the Maker of heaven and earth.*
>
> PSALM 121:1-2

Are you worried about making mistakes, disappointing your boss, or letting your family down? Memorize these words:

> *He will not let your foot slip—he who watches over you will not slumber; indeed, he who watches over Israel will neither slumber nor sleep.*
>
> PSALM 121:3-4

Does unnecessary anxiety sometimes get the best of you, causing you to fear for your own safety or health? Memorize these words:

> *The LORD watches over you—the LORD is your shade at your right hand; the sun will not harm you by day, nor the moon by night.*
>
> PSALM 121:5-6

✿

Are you already starting to agonize over next month's deadline, next year's taxes, the college tuition that has to be paid ten years from now, or funding your own retirement in thirty years? Are you taking all of that on when your head hits the pillow at night? Memorize these words:

> *The LORD will keep you from all harm—he will watch over your life; the LORD will watch over your coming and going both now and forevermore.*

> PSALM 121:7-8

You have just memorized an entire psalm! Repeat it to yourself every night. Substitute "my" for "your" and "me" for "you." Then rest in the knowledge that God has you, your life, and the rest of the universe under control.

———

MY SLEEP HAD BEEN PLEASANT TO ME.

JEREMIAH 31:26

❧ NOTES FROM CAMP ❧

Margaret Brownley tells of her son's first letters from camp: "When my oldest son went away to summer camp for the first time, I was a nervous wreck. Although he was nine years old, he hadn't as much as spent a night away from home, let alone an entire week. I packed his suitcase with special care, making sure he had enough socks and underwear to see him through the week. I also packed stationery and stamps so he could write home.

"I received the first letter from him three days after he left for camp. I quickly tore open the envelope and stared at the childish scrawl, which read: "Camp is fun, but the food is yucky!" The next letter offered little more: "Jerry wet the bed." *Who's Jerry?* I wondered. The third and final letter had this interesting piece of news: "The nurse said it's not broken."

"Fragments—bits of information that barely skim the surface. A preview of coming attractions that never materialize. It made me think of my own sparse messages to God. 'Dear Lord,' I plead when a son is late coming home, 'keep him safe.' Or, 'Give me strength,' I pray when faced with a difficult neighbor

❧

or the challenge of a checkbook run amuck. 'Let me have wisdom,' is another favorite prayer of mine, usually murmured in haste while waiting my turn at a parent/teacher conference or dealing with a difficult employee. 'Thank-you, God,' I say before each meal or when my brood is tucked in safely for the night.

"Fragments—bits and pieces. Are my messages to God as unsatisfactory to Him as my son's letters were to me? With a guilty start, I realized that it had been a long time since I'd had a meaningful chat with the Lord.

"When my son came home, he told me all about his adventures. It was good to have him home and safe. 'Thank-you, God,' I murmured, and then caught myself. It was time I sent God more than just a hasty note from 'camp.'"[33]

ONE DAY JESUS WAS PRAYING IN A
CERTAIN PLACE. WHEN HE FINISHED,
ONE OF HIS DISCIPLES SAID TO HIM,
"LORD, TEACH US TO PRAY."

LUKE 11:1

HOME SWEET HOME

Thoughts of "Home Sweet Home" don't usually conjure up high-tech images in our minds. But the new house of Microsoft CEO Bill Gates will have, not surprisingly, the latest in technological comforts and conveniences. When you enter his new house, you will receive an electronic pin to clip to your clothes. The pin identifies who and where you are and is programmed with your interests and tastes.

As you walk from room to room, the house adapts itself to your likes and dislikes. The temperature in each room automatically adjusts to your preference. The music you like will move with you from room to room. Digital images you want to see will appear on the walls of the rooms just before you enter and vanish after you leave.

What happens if there is more than one person in the room? No problem! The computer selects programming that suits both of your tastes![34]

Technology being what it is, someday we may all be able to customize our homes to respond to our most immediate interests, tastes, and comfort levels.

But there is something about the idea of "home" that goes well beyond the comfort and beauty of the physical surroundings. Home is a place where we can be ourselves. In that sense, there is a way in which no place on this planet will ever really be home for us.

George MacDonald in his work *Thomas Wingfold, Curate* said: "But there is that in us which is not at home in this world, which I believe holds secret relations with every star, or perhaps rather, with that in the heart of God whence issued every star. . . . To that in us, this world is so far strange and unnatural and unfitting, and we need a yet homelier home. Yea, no home at last will do, but the home of God's heart."

LORD, THOU HAST BEEN
OUR DWELLINGPLACE
IN ALL GENERATIONS.

PSALM 90:1 KJV

ᚱᚩ AFRAID OF THE DARK ᚱᚩ

At the turn of the century there was a city worker whose youth had been spent in evil ways. But one night during a revival meeting he was spiritually born anew. Soon after, he ran into one of his old drinking pals. Knowing his friend needed Jesus, he attempted to witness to him about his newly found peace. His friend rebuffed him rudely and made fun of him for "turning pious."

"I'll tell you what," said the new Christian. "You know that I am the city lamplighter. When I go 'round turning out the lights, I look back, and all the road over which I've been walking is blackness. That's what my past is like."

He went on, "I look on in front, and there's a long row of twinkling lights to guide me, and that's what the future is like since I found Jesus."

"Yes," said the friend, "but by-and-by you get to the last lamp and turn it out, and where are you then?"

"Then," said the Christian, "why, when the last lamp goes out it's dawn, and there ain't no need for lamps when the morning comes."

ᚱᚩ

Many children carry their fear of the dark into adulthood in the form of other kinds of fears—fear of failure, rejection, loss, pain, loneliness, or disappointment. Each of these fears seems to grow in darkness. Darkness is a metaphor for many things: death, night, uncertainty, evil—but in all of them, Jesus is the Light that brings illumination and comfort.

When light shines, not only is darkness eliminated, but fears are relieved. Indeed, not only does Jesus give you as much light as you need to proceed in faith, but because of His sacrifice at Calvary, you can be assured of His eternal dawn when the last lamp goes out! Like the lamplighter said, "There ain't no need for lamps when the morning comes."

═══════

YOU ARE A CHOSEN PEOPLE, A ROYAL PRIESTHOOD, A HOLY NATION, A PEOPLE BELONGING TO GOD, THAT YOU MAY DECLARE THE PRAISES OF HIM WHO CALLED YOU OUT OF DARKNESS INTO HIS WONDERFUL LIGHT.

1 PETER 2:9

❧ TIME TO REST ❧

What is it that gives you that warm fuzzy feeling inside? Certain smells, like the aroma of homemade bread right out of the oven or the cinnamony smell of hot apple cider, make you feel everything will be all right.

How about a crackling fire in the fireplace to chase away the damp chill on a rainy night? It makes you feel that life is good.

What about the whistling of a teakettle, ready to brew a pot of your favorite tea? Or listening to a favorite recording of Beethoven's "Moonlight Sonata"? When was the last time you sat outside to do nothing else but watch the sun set?

To Oscar Hammerstein, that warm, fuzzy, everything-is-going-to-be-okay feeling came from "whiskers on kittens and warm, woolen mittens." What are some of your favorite things?

When was the last time you gave yourself permission to be "nonproductive" and enjoy some of life's simple pleasures?

Logan Pearsall Smith wrote, "If you are losing your leisure, look out! You may be losing your soul."

❧

When we don't take time for leisure or relaxation, when we give our discretionary time away to busyness and relentless activity, we are living in a way that says, "Everything depends upon me and my efforts."

Consequently, God prescribed a day of rest, the Sabbath, to enjoy His creation, to give us time to reflect and remember all He has done for us and all He is. The Sabbath is time to remember that God is God—and we're not!

The Sabbath doesn't have to be Sunday. You can take a Sabbath rest anytime you relax and turn your focus to God and His creation. Sometimes you have nothing better to do than relax. You may have something *else* to do, but you don't have anything *better* to do.

Relax and just enjoy God's creation. After all, He created it for you to enjoy.

———————

BE GLAD AND REJOICE FOR EVER
IN THAT WHICH I CREATE.

ISAIAH 65:18 RSV

❧ ULTIMATE PEACE ❧

A word that appears throughout the Old
Testament is "shalom." It is often translated "peace,"
but shalom means far more than peace in the
aftermath of war or peace between enemies. Shalom
embodies an inner peace, which brings wholeness,
unity, and balance to an individual's life. It describes
a harmonious, nurturing environment, which has
God at its center.

In creation, God brought order and harmony
out of chaos. He created shalom. It was man's sin that
destroyed shalom, but it has always been God's plan
that it be restored—first to the human heart, and
flowing from that, heart-to-heart relationships.

In the book of Revelation, we have the glorious
hope that the Prince of Peace will rule over a new
heaven and earth that are described as perfect.
According to Isaiah, justice, righteousness, and peace
will characterize His unending kingdom. The Prince
of Shalom will restore God's original shalom!

God has given us many promises for peace in
His Word. Meditate on His promises of shalom, and

as you do, they will flood your heart and mind with peace, cleansing you from the stress of the day.

Therefore, since we have been justified through faith, we have peace with God through our Lord Jesus Christ (Romans 5:1).

Great peace have they who love your law, and nothing can make them stumble (Psalm 119:165).

When a man's ways are pleasing to the LORD, he makes even his enemies live at peace with him (Proverbs 16:7).

May the God of hope fill you with all joy and peace as you trust in him, so that you may overflow with hope (Romans 15:13).

And the peace of God, which transcends all understanding, will guard your hearts and your minds in Christ Jesus (Philippians 4:7).

You can have peace with God, peace in your walk, and peace with your enemies.

Shalom!

PEACE I LEAVE WITH YOU;
MY PEACE I GIVE YOU.

JOHN 14:27

❧ HEAVEN BOUND ❧

"If you read history you will find that the Christians who did most for the present world were just those who thought most of the next," wrote C. S. Lewis.

Recent research bears out this fact. Robert Wuthnow reports, "Christians are more likely to volunteer than other citizens, more prone to give significant time to caring for others, and more likely to believe that they have a duty to do so. Those who attend church regularly, who are active in fellowship and Bible-study groups, who gain a great deal of satisfaction from their religion are far more active volunteers than those who have little church involvement and gain little satisfaction from faith."

One reason why Christians are likely to be involved in helping others is they don't see life on earth as the sum total of their existence. In fact, this life is simply an opportunity to do good.

Christians are actually citizens of another place— Heaven. They are persons whose Father is in Heaven; their treasure and home are in Heaven. They are born from above, and their affections and attention are set on things above. As citizens of heaven, they

are ambassadors who represent the kingdom of
Heaven on earth.

What does it mean to be an ambassador?

↬ *An ambassador is a representative.*

↬ *An ambassador is a foreigner in the country where
he or she is living.*

↬ *An ambassador is only a temporary resident of the
country where he or she is living.*

↬ *An ambassador always keeps in mind the one he or
she serves; that is an ambassador's purpose.*

↬ *An ambassador will assist those who wish to
immigrate to his or her country.*

Turn your thoughts toward Heaven before
sleeping tonight. See how it changes your perspective
about your life on earth.

WE ARE HIS WORKMANSHIP, CREATED
IN CHRIST JESUS FOR GOOD WORKS,
WHICH GOD PREPARED BEFOREHAND,
THAT WE SHOULD WALK IN THEM.

EPHESIANS 2:10 RSV

⊷ PATIENCE PAYS ⊷

David and Lynn were getting discouraged. The restaurant they owned was foundering even though they had extended their business hours and offered special dinners, hoping to attract more customers. But no one came.

After several weeks with no change in sight, Lynn said, "We might as well close up and go on home." It was nearly eleven o'clock.

"Let's stay open a few more hours," David suggested.

"Why?" Lynn frowned. "What's the use?"

"Because tonight may be the night we get more customers." David grinned, and his wife noticed the hope shining in his large hazel eyes.

Even though Lynn didn't relish the idea, she agreed that they should keep the restaurant open.

About thirty minutes later, a miracle seemed to occur. A late evening bus drove into the small community and stopped in front of the café. People poured out of the bus and into the cold winter air. Quickly they entered the warm café, since it was the only restaurant still open.

The profits David and Lynn made that evening helped compensate for some of their earlier losses. But that was only the beginning.

⊷

Soon word spread that the small restaurant stayed open late at night. Business came from all around—people driving through the town late at night, buses passing through, late-night railroad crews. The couple even had to hire an extra waitress for the late shift.

Sometimes when we've worked late into the night and are ready to give up, if we wait patiently, we will reach our goals. What we long for may arrive within minutes. Take comfort in the fact that we don't know what tomorrow brings. It could be a special day—or night—for us.

SIMON ANSWERED, "MASTER, WE'VE WORKED HARD ALL NIGHT AND HAVEN'T CAUGHT ANYTHING. BUT BECAUSE YOU SAY SO, I WILL LET DOWN THE NETS." WHEN THEY HAD DONE SO, THEY CAUGHT SUCH A LARGE NUMBER OF FISH THAT THEIR NETS BEGAN TO BREAK.

LUKE 5:5-6

Evangelist and singer N. B. Vandall sat quietly in his living room reading his paper when one of his sons rushed into the house, crying, "Paul is hurt! A car hit him and dragged him down the street! He was bleeding all over, and somebody came and took him away."

Vandall found his son at a nearby hospital with serious head injuries, a concussion, and multiple broken bones. The surgeon did not know if he would live. All the distraught father could do was pray as the doctor cleaned and stitched Paul's head wounds and set his broken bones. The rest was up to God.

After coming home to give his family the report, Vandall returned to the living room and fell on his knees with a heartfelt cry of, "O God!" Almost immediately, Vandall could hear God's voice inside him, telling him that no matter what happened in the here and now, all tears will be dried and sorrows will cease in the hereafter. Vandall went to the piano and in minutes wrote a hymn titled "After."

After the toil and the heat of the day,
After my troubles are past,
After the sorrows are taken away,

I shall see Jesus at last.
He will be waiting for me—
Jesus so kind and true;
On His beautiful throne,
He will welcome me home—
After the day is through.

Paul had a near perfect recovery from his injuries, and his father's faith in God remained strong and steady, his gratitude boundless.[35]

God wants to be with you in the midst of your tribulations, too, putting a song of praise in your mouth. When you turn your focus from your struggles to Him, His awesome power can overcome whatever you are facing.

———

HE PUT A NEW SONG IN MY MOUTH,
A HYMN OF PRAISE TO OUR GOD.
MANY WILL SEE AND FEAR, AND
PUT THEIR TRUST IN THE LORD.

PSALM 40:3

↬ WHY WORRY? ↫

Many people lose sleep by worrying. They lie awake in bed, wondering if they made a right decision the day before—if they did the wrong thing—and what they should do tomorrow.

Here's a creative way one woman handled worry. With so many things to worry about, she decided to set aside one day each week to worry. As worrying situations occurred, she wrote them down and put them in her worry box. Then, on Worry Wednesday, she read through each worry. To her amazement, most of the things she was disturbed about had already been taken care of in some way. Thus, she learned there was seldom a justifiable reason to worry. As the psalmist wrote in Psalm 127:2 NKJV, *It is vain for you to rise up early, to sit up late, to eat the bread of sorrows; for so He gives His beloved sleep.*

American poet Ellen M. Huntington Gates described God's perfect rest for those with weary hearts in her poem "Sleep Sweet."

> *Sleep sweet within this quiet room,*
> *O thou, whoe'er thou art,*
> *And let no mournful yesterdays*
> *Disturb thy peaceful heart.*

↬↫

Nor let tomorrow mar thy rest
With dreams of coming ill:
Thy Maker is thy changeless friend,
His love surrounds thee still.
Forget thyself and all the world,
Put out each garish light:
The stars are shining overhead
Sleep sweet! Good night! Good night![36]

As a child of God, you can rest in the knowledge that you are surrounded by a loving Father who cares for you. Jesus said, "'Look at the birds of the air, for they neither sow nor reap nor gather into barns; yet your heavenly Father feeds them. Are you not of more value than they?'" (Matthew 6:26 NKJV). Trust in God without fear or anxiety about what tomorrow may bring. The same Creator who placed each star in the sky is watching over you.

"THEREFORE DO NOT WORRY ABOUT
TOMORROW, FOR TOMORROW WILL
WORRY ABOUT ITS OWN THINGS.
SUFFICIENT FOR THE DAY
IS ITS OWN TROUBLE."

MATTHEW 6:34 NKJV

MADE FOR
~ ANOTHER WORLD ~

"Satisfaction guaranteed!" promise the ads for a new car, a refreshing soft drink, or a stay at an exotic resort. There is no end to the commercial world's promises of fulfilled hopes and dreams.

Do you know many truly satisfied people? Would you describe our culture as satisfied?

If you answer no, you're not alone. Author Max Lucado doesn't think so either. He said, "That is one thing we are not. We are not satisfied. . . ."

After Thanksgiving dinner we declare, "I'm satisfied." In reality, we are probably more than satisfied! But before the end of the day's football games, we are back in the kitchen digging into the leftovers.

We plan and save for years for the "perfect vacation." We head off to our dream-come-true destination, indulge every desire for fun, food, and fantasy, and in two weeks we are headed home with wonderful memories. It may have been a satisfying two weeks, but are we fulfilled for the rest of our lives when the vacation is over?

~

Perhaps you worked to build the home of your dreams—the place where you are king and reign over every affordable luxury and creature comfort. Does it truly satisfy your deepest desires?

Satisfaction is hard to obtain. Contentment eludes us. We are promised fulfillment many times a day, but the promises become empty after we have "taken the bite" a few times. There is nothing on earth that can satisfy our deepest longing.

In *Mere Christianity,* C.S. Lewis wrote: "If I find in myself a desire which no experience in this world can satisfy, the most probable explanation is that I was made for another world."

We were made for another world—Heaven! The desire for satisfaction is very strong in our lives. However, Scripture tells us there is only one thing that will satisfy: "In him we live and move and have our being. As some of your own poets have said, We are his offspring" (Acts 17:28).

IN YOUR PRESENCE IS
FULLNESS OF JOY.

PSALM 16:11 NKJV

❧ WINTER STORM ❧

Elizabeth stared out the window at the low-hanging rain clouds. Kissing the top of her newborn's head, she snugly wrapped the blanket around him, wishing her husband were home. The child opened his slate-blue eyes and cooed. As her heart filled with love for this new human being, she felt an inexplicable warmth pass between them. She wondered if perhaps this was the way God felt about His children.

By nighttime the rain had turned into a tap-tapping sound, and Elizabeth realized it was now sleeting outside.

"I'll bet you want something to eat," she said, touching the baby's cheek. She placed him on his side in the playpen and gave him a warmed bottle, then began to pace the floor.

Later, the sleet turned to freezing rain. Peeking outside, she could see the ice-coated pine trees bowing to their knees. Nervously, she said out loud, "Jim, where are you?"

Just as she started toward the telephone, the lights went out. She lit the Christmas candle on the mantel. The house quickly chilled. She wrapped another blanket around the baby and put a cap on his head, then pulled on her coat.

What if the lights don't come back on soon? What if they don't come on for days? Her mind raced through all the possibilities. Where was her husband? In all this bad weather, had he been in an accident? "Oh, Lord," she whispered, "I'm so afraid."

In the darkness and deepening silence, she heard an inner voice remind her that God is our refuge and strength, an ever-present help in trouble. Within the hour her husband came home, and not long after that the lights blinked on.

God says in His Word, the Bible, that we should not give in to our fears, but we often do. This night, cast your doubts and fears at the foot of the Cross, and let the outstretched arms of Jesus Christ wrap you in His peace.

―――

GOD DID NOT GIVE US A SPIRIT OF TIMIDITY, BUT A SPIRIT OF POWER, OF LOVE AND OF SELF-DISCIPLINE.

2 TIMOTHY 1:7

One of the translations for the word "meditate" in Hebrew, the language in which the Old Testament was written, is the verb "to mutter"—to voice under one's breath, to continually repeat something. When we are taught to meditate upon the Lord and His Word day and night, we are to repeat God's Word to ourselves continually. When we do this, God's Word becomes foremost in our thinking. It becomes our mind-set, our worldview, our perspective on life.

The Scriptures promise that when we think and speak in accordance with God's law, we will act accordingly. Thus we will enjoy success and prosperity!

In the opinion of Henry Ward Beecher, a great preacher from the 1800s, "A few moments with God at that calm and tranquil season are of more value than much fine gold."

The psalmist proclaimed, "My mouth shall praise thee with joyful lips: when I remember thee upon my bed, and meditate on thee in the night watches" (Psalm 63:5-6 KJV).

Have your last conscious thoughts before sleeping be about God's Word. Turn off the late show, close the novel, put away the work, and rest in the Lord, recalling His Word. You'll find it easier to do this if you choose a passage of Scripture on which to meditate in the morning and then meditate upon it all day— muttering phrases and verses to yourself in the odd moments of your schedule. Then, just before you fall asleep, remind yourself one final time of God's truth.

Those who do this report a more restful night. A peaceful mind focused on God's Word seems to produce peaceful sleep and deep relaxation for the body. In this day and age, with nearly a billion dollars spent each year on sleep aids, we have the greatest sleep aid of all—the Word of God!

———

THIS BOOK OF THE LAW SHALL NOT DEPART OUT OF THY MOUTH; BUT THOU SHALT MEDITATE THEREIN DAY AND NIGHT, THAT THOU MAYEST OBSERVE TO DO ACCORDING TO ALL THAT IS WRITTEN THEREIN: FOR THEN THOU SHALT MAKE THY WAY PROSPEROUS, AND THEN THOU SHALT HAVE GOOD SUCCESS.

JOSHUA 1:8 KJV

❧ A SONG OF HOPE ❧

During a time of unbelievable tragedy, Horatio Gates Spafford wrote a song of hope and faith. Spafford, a deeply spiritual man, built a successful law practice in Chicago just after the Civil War. He had five children: four girls and a boy. But like Job, Spafford endured great hardships.

Spafford's young son died of pneumonia. Four months later, Spafford lost all of his property and wealth in the Great Chicago Fire. After so much distress, Spafford's family planned a trip to join his good friend, Dwight L. Moody, in Great Britain. But unfinished business forced Spafford to stay behind while his wife and daughters went ahead by ship. On that voyage, Spafford lost all four daughters in a shipwreck, with only his wife surviving.

It was while sailing to join his wife that he received the inspiration for his greatest work and testimony. Looking out from the ship at the site where his daughters had drowned, he thought he couldn't bear any more pain. Then he recalled this Scripture: "For God so loved the world that He gave His only begotten Son" (John 3:16 KJV). Spafford realized that he would see his children again. Praying with a heart filled with that hope, Spafford uttered, "Whatever my lot, it is well with my soul."

Spafford put his thoughts on paper. After he and his wife returned home from Europe, Philip P. Bliss composed a tune to accompany Spafford's poem. The result is one of the best-loved hymns of all time.

If you think you cannot bear any more pain and feel all is lost, remember that God gave all He had and knows what you are facing. Read this beloved hymn and know that it is well with your soul:

> When peace, like a river, attendeth my way,
> When sorrows like sea billows roll
> Whatever my lot, Thou hast taught me to say,
> It is well, it is well with my soul.[37]

WHEN I LIE DOWN, I SAY,
WHEN SHALL I ARISE, AND THE
NIGHT BE GONE? AND I AM FULL
OF TOSSINGS TO AND FRO UNTO
THE DAWNING OF THE DAY.

JOB 7:4 KJV

"Oh, no! We're going to have to run for the ferry again!" Elaine cried. "And, unless we find a parking place in the next minute or two, we're never going to make it!"

As Elaine and her daughter, Cathy, struggled through the downtown Seattle traffic, she thought back to when they had moved to Bainbridge Island four years earlier. They had thought it to be a perfect, idyllic place, her daughter was in high school, and she could work part-time at home.

Now college bills had made full-time work a necessity for Elaine. She, her husband, and Cathy were obliged to make the daily commute to Seattle via the ferry. With a car parked on both sides of the water, praying for parking spaces had become a daily event.

"I told you we needed to get away from your office sooner," Cathy chided. "You just can't count on finding a parking place within walking distance of the ferry when the waterfront is full of summer tourists and conventioneers!"

"God knew about the last-minute customer I had, and He knows we have to make this ferry in order to get home in time to fix dinner and make it to the church meeting," Elaine assured her. Then she prayed aloud, "Lord, we'll circle this block one more time. Please have someone back out, or we're not going to make it."

"Mom, there it is!" Cathy shouted, as they rounded the last corner. "Those people just got in their car. I have to admit—sometimes you have a lot more faith than I do. Who'd think God would be interested in whether we find a parking place?"

"But that's the exciting part of it," Elaine explained. "God is interested in every part of our lives—even schedules and parking places. Now, let's run for it!"[38]

The Lord knows all the circumstances of your day—and your tomorrow. Trust Him to be the "Lord of the details."

———

THIS IS THE CONFIDENCE WE HAVE IN APPROACHING GOD: THAT IF WE ASK ANYTHING ACCORDING TO HIS WILL, HE HEARS US. AND IF WE KNOW THAT HE HEARS US — WHATEVER WE ASK — WE KNOW THAT WE HAVE WHAT WE ASKED OF HIM.

1 JOHN 5:14-15

↬ THE HEALING TREE ↫

Writer Marion Bond West wrote about "The Healing Tree" when things weren't going right and she doubted her roles as wife and mother. At the time, her self-reliant older daughter was pregnant, she and her teenage daughter couldn't seem to get along, and the twin boys preferred their father.

One afternoon, she asked her husband if he wanted to go for a walk. "No," he said in a matter-of-fact way.

Disappointed, West drove to the woods and walked by herself. The only sounds were her own footsteps and rushing water in a stream. In the distance, she saw a lone black walnut tree. At its base, she sat down. The wind churned, and leaves detached from a branch. *How easily this tree lets those leaves go,* she said to herself. *If only I could let go as easily.*

Thinking of her husband, West picked up a branch. She prayed to release those things about him that troubled her and tossed the stick into the water. Picking up a smaller stick, she thought, *Please let me stop controlling my daughter's life.* She threw the stick as far as she could.

One by one, she released her children to the Lord. A larger stick represented her pregnant daughter. *Don't let me be meddlesome in her affairs, Lord.* She dropped the stick into the water.

Then she picked up twin sticks. *Don't let me press the boys into what I think they should be,* she prayed, tossing both sticks into the swirling water.

The last stick was hers. *Lord,* she prayed, *there's so much in me that is selfish and demanding. Love my family with Your unconditional love.* She dropped her stick into the stream. Immediately, she felt a sense of freedom from her bondage of worry.

There's freedom in releasing our loved ones to the Lord. When we stop clinging to past anger and disappointment, we experience the Lord's unfailing love and acceptance.[39]

THE LORD DELIGHTS IN THOSE WHO FEAR HIM, WHO PUT THEIR HOPE IN HIS UNFAILING LOVE.

PSALM 147:11

❧ FINDING IT ALL ❧

They were married as soon as they graduated
from college. They both were smart, attractive, and
voted by their peers as "most likely to succeed".
Within two decades, they had reached some pretty
lofty rungs on the ladder of success: three children
who attended private schools, a mansion, two luxury
cars, a vacation house on the lake, a prolific
investment portfolio, and the respect of all who knew
them. If you had asked them what was most important
in life, they would have reeled off a list of all they
owned, the places they had been, and the things they
had done. Success was sweet, and money made their
world go round.

It will probably come as no surprise to you to
learn that one day the bottom dropped out of this
couple's life. They had personally guaranteed a
business loan, assuming that their partners were as
trustworthy as they. Not so. One partner embezzled
nearly half a million dollars, and this Couple-Who-
Had-It-All started down the road to becoming the
Couple-Who-Lost-It-All. In the midst of their
problems, the police came to their door late one

❧

night to tell them their oldest son had been killed in a car accident.

This couple discovered something vitally important in the course of putting their lives back together. A neighbor invited them to church, and thinking that they had nothing to lose by going, they started attending, eventually becoming regular members. To their amazement, they found they were enjoying Bible study, making lots of genuine friends, and feeling accepted for who they were—not for what they had in the way of material possessions. Their children also found a place to belong (no designer jeans required).[40]

Ideally, we don't have to lose it all in order to find it all. In fact, our Heavenly Father wants us to live abundantly. Keeping our priorities straight, remembering to put God first and others ahead of ourselves, is the key to sweet sleep at night!

DON'T STORE UP TREASURES
ON EARTH!

MATTHEW 6:19 CEV

Stressed to the max nearly every evening after a busy day caring for her two preschoolers, Samantha would crawl into bed at night, feeling as if she hadn't accomplished anything. Before marriage, she had worked as an accountant in one of the firms downtown. Now she was a harried mother.

In contrast, her husband's career was flourishing. She was happy about his success, but at the same time she felt unimportant in comparison to him. While she spent the day chasing toddlers, her husband consulted with corporate presidents and designed skyscrapers.

"I envy you," Samantha said one night.

Kent's dark eyebrows shot up in surprise. "Why on earth would you be jealous of me?"

"Because you're so successful. Every day I do the same boring things. I don't do anything that's important."

"But you do so much!"

"Like what? Change dirty diapers?" Samantha felt even sorrier for herself.

Kent pointed out to his wife that every day she spent quality time with their children by reading them Bible stories, taking them swimming or to the library, making play dough, cooking three nutritious meals, and bathing them. On top of that, Kent continued, she also volunteered her time in the church nursery.

"Don't you think those things count?" he asked.

Samantha admitted that she had never thought about her life in that way. Instead of focusing on the joys of the present, she had mourned for the life she had left behind. That night, instead of going to sleep right away, she reflected on what her husband had said. She could always resume her career when the kids went off to school. God seemed to say, *Enjoy your family now while you can. Your children won't be little forever.*

Tonight you can do the same. Think of all the contributions you are making to others. And then sleep in peace, knowing that God is pleased with you.

I STAY AWAKE THROUGH THE NIGHT
TO THINK ABOUT YOUR PROMISES.

PSALM 119:148 TLB

ᜒ GRACIOUS LIGHT ᜒ

The *Book of Common Prayer* has a service of Evening
Prayer, which includes an ancient hymn called "Phos
hilararon" or "O Gracious Light:"

O gracious Light, pure brightness of the everliving Father
  in heaven,
O Jesus Christ, holy and blessed!

Now as we come to the setting of the sun,
and our eyes behold the vesper light,
we sing your praises, O God:
Father, Son, and Holy Spirit.

You are worthy at all times to be praised by happy voices,
O Son of God, O Giver of life,
and to be glorified through all the worlds.

This ancient hymn calls our attention to the fact
that although the sun may be going down, God's light
never leaves us. He is with us always, day and night.

Ancient pagans believed that night was a time of
death and sadness, of a "departure of the gods" from
the world. This hymn proclaims the exact opposite.
Jesus Christ gives life around the clock. The Father
never abandons His children, and He is worthy of
praise at all times.

ᜒ

In the book of Revelation, John describes the New Jerusalem, our eternal home, with these words:

There shall be no night there; and they need no candle, neither light of the sun; for the Lord God giveth them light; and they shall reign for ever and ever.

REVELATION 22:5 KJV

Scientists today tell us if anything is reduced to its purest form of energy, it becomes light and heat—the sun in miniature. The gospel tells us the Son of God is our unending supply of energy and life.

He is who and what nothing else can provide! He is the essence of all of life's energy. You can count on Him to bring light, even in your darkest night.

GOD IS LIGHT, AND IN HIM IS NO DARKNESS AT ALL.

1 JOHN 1:5 KJV

Janelle became so distraught with the stress of deadlines in her work as an artist that she didn't know what to do. She decided to call her friend, Gail.

"Hello," Gail answered. At the sound of her voice, Janelle burst into tears.

"What's wrong?" Gail asked.

"Could you come over? I'm so depressed," Janelle said.

"Of course."

Within a few minutes, Gail sat on the edge of Janelle's bed. Janelle noticed that Gail held a book in her hands.

"What's that?" Janelle asked.

"A joke book."

"I'm not in the mood for jokes," Janelle said.

"Let me read you just one," Gail suggested.

Janelle wasn't excited about the idea, but she agreed to listen to one joke. Gail read the joke, and Janelle couldn't help but laugh.

Smiling, Gail's dark blonde eyebrows raised as she asked, "Can I read another one?"

Janelle shrugged. "I guess it can't hurt anything. You might as well go ahead."

So Gail read another joke. Janelle laughed again.

This continued until Gail had read about a dozen jokes. The laughter brought Janelle out of her depression. After Gail left, Janelle returned to her paintings with a renewed vigor.

Laughter is a gift from God to help us through the hard times in life. When we laugh, our bodies release endorphins, a substance that produces calmness in much the same way as a tranquilizer. That's why so many doctors say laughter is a great healing tool for the troubled soul. What a blessing we can be to others by sharing the gift of laughter!

A CHEERFUL HEART IS GOOD
MEDICINE, BUT A CRUSHED
SPIRIT DRIES UP THE BONES.

PROVERBS 17:22

IN HIS PRESENCE

Once there was a widow who lived in a miserable attic with her son. Years before, the woman had married against her parents' wishes and had gone to live in a foreign land with her husband.

Her husband had proved irresponsible and unfaithful, and after a few years he died without having made any provision for her and their child. It was with the utmost difficulty that she managed to scrape together the bare necessities of life.

The happiest times in the child's life were when the mother took him in her arms and told him about her father's house in the old country. She told him of the grassy lawn, the noble trees, the wild flowers, the lovely paintings, and the delicious meals.

The child had never seen his grandfather's home, but to him it was the most beautiful place in the entire world. He longed for the time when he would go to live there.

One day the postman knocked at the attic door. The mother recognized the handwriting on the envelope, and with trembling fingers she broke the seal. There was a check and a slip of paper with just two words: "Come home."[41]

Like this father—and the father of the prodigal son—our Heavenly Father opens His arms to receive us back into a place of spiritual comfort and restoration at the end of a weary day.

God does not ask us to stand and take our punishment for the day's failures. He simply welcomes us into His presence as children redeemed by the blood of His Son. There, He assures us that He understands our hurts and shortcomings and—miracle of all miracles—loves us anyway.

The Father is calling you to come home. Why not finish your day in the comfort and provision of His presence?

———

THIS SON OF MINE WAS DEAD
AND IS ALIVE AGAIN; HE WAS
LOST AND IS FOUND.

LUKE 15:24

❧ CLEARING THE CLUTTER ❧

As Angela cleaned her house one weekend, she wondered why on earth she kept so much stuff around that had to be picked up, dusted, or maintained in some other way. She spent hours during the week picking up papers, magazines, the television guide, and mail that hadn't been dealt with, along with the usual vacuuming, mopping, and laundering. She began thinking of ways to simplify her house to make her life easier at night and on weekends and free up more time to spend with her family. She vowed to stop letting clutter rule her life.

As she lay in bed thinking of ways to do this, Angela realized that her thought processes were as cluttered as the physical portion of her life. She recognized that she tended to rationalize, procrastinate, and fill up her mind with excuses to delay making important decisions. Her relationships with her husband and children were suffering because of all the emotional clutter filling up her heart. She never seemed to have enough time to spend with God. Angela had to admit to herself that clutter ruled her life. So she prayed and asked God to reorder her life.

Gradually, He helped her to clear away the years of clutter in her mind, emotions, and in her house. Instead of making excuses, she took time to read to her children and attend their school functions. Her husband benefited from a more loving and relaxed wife.

Think about ways you can clear up the clutter in your life. Use the extra time to create close, loving relationships with God and your family. Without all the clutter, it will be much easier to see the plan God has for you and to make your decisions in a way that is pleasing to Him.

THEN YOU WILL CALL UPON ME AND COME AND PRAY TO ME, AND I WILL LISTEN TO YOU. YOU WILL SEEK ME AND FIND ME WHEN YOU SEEK ME WITH ALL YOUR HEART.

JEREMIAH 29:12-13

❧ A HEALTHY HABIT ❧

Most of us are familiar with the old saying: "Early to bed and early to rise, makes a man healthy and wealthy and wise." And there are numerous references in the Bible to the joys and benefits of rising early. The psalmist said,

> *My heart is steadfast, O God, my heart is steadfast;*
> *I will sing and give praise. Awake, my glory!*
> *Awake, lute and harp! I will awaken the dawn.*
>
> PSALM 57:7-8 NKJV

The clear implication is that the psalmist had a habit of getting up before dawn and "singing in" the morning. But what does this have to do with our sunset hours?

Very practically speaking, in order to be able to rise early in the morning, we have to go to bed early. There is no substitute for sleep. According to modern sleep research, most people need seven to ten hours of sleep a day, and lost hours can never be made up.

Sufficient sleep is the foremost factor in a person's ability to sustain a high performance level, cope with stress, and feel a sense of satisfaction in

❧

life. Getting enough sleep directly affects our moods and emotions and our ability to sustain exertion. It is as vital to our health as what we eat and drink.

More good news about sleep and our health is that every hour of sleep we get before midnight is twice as beneficial as the hours after midnight!

A good night's sleep is one of God's blessings to you. Sufficient sleep was part of His design for your body and His plan for your life. When you make a habit of retiring early, you put yourself in a position to receive this blessing. You'll find it easier to rise early and seek the Lord for wisdom and strength for the day ahead.

O GOD, YOU ARE MY GOD;
EARLY WILL I SEEK YOU.

PSALM 63:1 NKJV

❧ ONE FOOT IN FRONT ❧
OF THE OTHER

In the early 1960s, Jason was working in Oregon. One day in the winter, he took a group of young people from his church to hike in the mountains. Their parents were to pick them up at an old schoolhouse at two o'clock.

The sky was clear when they set out. But around noon, snow began to fall, and soon they could see no more than ten feet in front of them. Jason prayed for guidance and strength, then told the young people to hold on to one another. He urged them not to be afraid but to put one foot in front of the other and to keep praying. Slowly, they moved forward. After what seemed like hours, they finally made it down the mountain and found themselves not far from the school.

Jason visited the Hood River Valley again in 1992, where he met a woman from the church he had attended. She still remembered the expedition and told him that her memory of praying and putting one foot in front of the other had been an image that had guided her through many of life's stormy days.[42]

During our lifetime, we make millions of decisions. Some are small. Others are major, life-changing decisions regarding marriage, jobs, and education. We make most of these decisions based on the best information we have available at the time.

If you take your choices to the Lord and lay them before Him, He will help you to know what is in your heart and what your reasons are for making a decision. Some individuals are so afraid of making the wrong decision that they do nothing. Living your life to the fullest means communicating with God on a daily basis and continuing to put one foot in front of the other—regardless of the obstacles.

COMMIT YOUR WAY TO THE LORD; TRUST IN HIM, AND HE WILL ACT.

PSALM 37:5 NRSV

❧ TAKING THE HARD ROAD ❧

Václav Havel is a former president of what used to be Czechoslovakia. In 1948 the Communists took power in his country and confiscated his family's land holdings. From that time, Havel was part of a defiant underground that opposed the Soviet government.

When the Soviets marched into Prague twenty years later, Havel remained to form a coalition that would gather strength and be ready to take over when the time was right. He spoke out boldly, writing defiantly against communism. He was put under surveillance and eventually jailed for his activities.

In 1970 several U.S. senators met with Havel in Czechoslovakia. They brought what they thought would be good news for him. They told him they intended to press for legislation allowing dissidents like him to emigrate to the West.

Havel replied by saying he was not interested in going to the West. "What good would that do?" he asked. "Only by staying here and struggling here can we ever hope to change things." Like a watchman in the night, Havel stayed on duty in his country.

Times of trial and struggle often seem like long, dark nights. But doing the right thing—even the hard thing—gives us hope. How do we maintain those long night watches when there seems to be little change in our circumstances?

1. Take one step at a time. Don't attempt to tackle the whole task at once. *A man's steps are directed by the LORD* (Proverbs 20:24).

2. Keep your struggles in perspective. Separate the mountains from the molehills. *What then shall we say in response to this? If God is for us, who can be against us?* (Romans 8:31).

3. Cultivate the discipline of delayed gratification. *Let patience have her perfect work, that ye may be perfect and entire, wanting nothing* (James 1:4 KJV).

4. Learn to recognize the invisible God in the world around you. *By faith he [Moses] left Egypt, not fearing the king's anger; he persevered because he saw him who is invisible* (Hebrews 11:27).[43]

Placing your hope in the Lord helps you to do all these things. He will lead you; He will remove your mountains; He will strengthen you, helping you to be patient; and He will open your eyes to His works all around you.

YOU ARE MY HOPE, O LORD GOD.

PSALM 71:5 NKJV

❧ I LOVE YOU ❧

"Don't stand so tall, Daddy," the little freckle-faced boy cried in the grocery store aisle. No matter how many times he pulled on his father's pants leg, he couldn't get any attention. Tears rolled down his face, as his father seemed to ignore his pleas.

"Don't stand so tall, Daddy!" he cried again, but much louder this time. The man finally leaned down in front of his son and looked at him eye to eye, listening intently. A smile lit up the little boy's face, replacing his tears.

The child reached out and held his father's face with his little hands. "I love you, Daddy," he said.

"I love you too, son," his father said simply.

The man stood up and resumed his shopping. Happy and content, the little boy followed in his father's footsteps. He had only needed the assurance of those special words—*I love you.* He wanted to know for sure that his father loved him.

How many times have we simply needed someone to offer a kind word or a gentle hug to get us through a trying situation? When insecurities arise or when our days abruptly turn to night, those three little words can mean so much. *I love you!* We all need our loved ones to come down to our level where we can confide in them.

Even though God is all-powerful and stands tall over our world, when we call upon His name, He reaches down and communicates with us heart to heart. He shows His love for us through His Word, in the beauty of the universe, and in the miracle of life. When we kneel in prayer, God's Spirit draws near to us to whisper those special words—*I love you.* We never grow too old to appreciate the assurance of His love.

HOW GREAT IS THE LOVE THE FATHER HAS LAVISHED ON US, THAT WE SHOULD BE CALLED CHILDREN OF GOD!

1 JOHN 3:1

❧ A BEAUTIFUL FINISH ❧

Putting the finish on a piece of furniture is the final step in its construction. The bulk of the work that gives the chest, table, or chair its *function* happens much earlier in the process. But it is the finish—the staining and varnishing—that very often gives a piece of furniture its *beauty*. The finish brings out the grain and luster of the wood, the smoothness of the craftsmanship, and the shine that speaks of completion.

The cross on which Jesus was crucified marked the end of His earthly life. As He exhaled His last breath, He declared, "It is finished." This was a triumphant statement that marked the completion of His earthly mission to satisfy and fulfill God's law for all mankind. The cross became the beacon that shines brightly into sinful hearts and says, "You can be free." It also became the prelude for a "new beginning" at His resurrection—offering new life for all.

We are each called to end our lives well, but our finish is not simply at our death. It is also in our bringing closure to each day in such a way that we allow for our resurrection the following morning. It is saying with thankfulness and humility, "I've done what the Lord put before me to do today, to the best of my ability. And now, I give my all to Him anew so that He might recreate me and use me again tomorrow."

Ralph Waldo Emerson offered this advice: "Finish every day and be done with it. You have done what you could. Some blunders and absurdities no doubt crept in; forget them as soon as you can. Tomorrow is a new day; begin it well and serenely and with too high a spirit to be cumbered with your old nonsense. This day is all that is good and fair. It is too dear, with its hopes and invitations, to waste a moment on yesterdays."

Amen! The God who began a good work in you will finish it day by day and ultimately bring it to completion. (See Philippians 1:6.)

AS HE HAD BEGUN, SO HE
WOULD ALSO COMPLETE
THIS GRACE IN YOU.

2 CORINTHIANS 8:6 NKJV

❧ A SERVICE OF LOVE ❧

Sam's wife hadn't attended a worship service for more than thirty years. Sunday after Sunday, the elderly deacon walked in and found his seat alone on the second pew. Newcomers thought he was single, but the established members knew the truth. He was a dedicated soul who lived his life serving and praising His Father in heaven. He passed out candy to the little ones and expressed his love freely among the members of the quaint church.

Although his wife, Helen, wasn't present during the worship service, she was there in spirit with her husband. She also supported the pastor with her prayers and fattened him up with her delightful chocolate desserts. Over the chatter of little mouths and the screaming of infants, she faithfully listened to his sermons by intercom.

Sam and Helen were always the first ones to arrive for every service. Helen had an important job to do and took it quite seriously. As director of the church nursery, she wanted to be early and ready before the little ones arrived. Each and every day of the week, she lifted her babies up in prayer before

❧

she retired for the night. She loved each special one as if it were her own.

Many women offered to relieve her, but she wouldn't allow it. God had called her to this service, and it was her intention to continue with it as long as possible. Over the years, "her" babies grew to adulthood and presented her with children of their own. She was truly loved by all.

As she rocked and sang to each child, she was serving her God in a powerful way. She provided a safe and warm environment for the little ones, while their parents fed on the Word of God.

God has a job for each of us. This woman found hers in the care of tiny babies. Tonight, ask God how you can serve Him best.

"WHOEVER WELCOMES A
LITTLE CHILD LIKE THIS IN
MY NAME WELCOMES ME."

MATTHEW 18:5

TIMELESS PEACE

In the midst of violence, terror, or war, is it possible to find an island of peace? Where does one go to experience tranquility?

The one place no one would expect to find peace is in the court of the Yugoslav War Crimes Tribunal, convened in The Hague. Certainly the president of that court needed some way to escape from the horrible stories that were crossing his desk regarding Bosnia.

How did Antonio Cassese supplant the gruesome images of man's inhumanity? By paying a visit to the Mauritshuis Museum in the center of town and filling his head with the beautiful images of paintings by Johannes Vermeer.

What is it about Vermeer that inspired Cassese? He says it was the peacefulness and serenity of the works.

Peace and serenity? Those are hardly words that Vermeer knew! He lived in Europe during a period of tumult and conflict. England and the United Provinces of the Netherlands, Vermeer's homeland, were at war three times during his forty-two years. Vermeer also had many children, numerous debts, and suffered a humiliating bankruptcy. How could his paintings embody peace? The following story gives us a clue.

During a political crisis some years back, a young man and several of his compatriots had allowed themselves to become overwrought about the situation in their homeland. A historian from England spoke with the group and reminded them of the story of Jesus calming the water. (See Matthew 8:23-27.) "It seems to me," this historian said, "that in the midst of a storm, you shouldn't let the tumult enter you. The thing to do is get in touch with the peace that resides inside you and let it out."

Vermeer tapped into a peace he harbored inside himself and shared it with others through his paintings. Cassese was receiving that same peace from his paintings many years later.[44]

The peace inside you has a powerful name—Jesus. Keep your mind on Him tonight, and watch the storms of your life fade into the background.

YOU WILL KEEP IN PERFECT PEACE
HIM WHOSE MIND IS STEADFAST.

ISAIAH 26:3

❧ THE KEY ❧

The school custodian looked like a very important man to the young boy. "Mr. Jones has more keys than anyone I know," he told his teacher one beautiful spring day. He was amazed at all the keys that Mr. Jones carried on his belt.

"He *is* an important man," his teacher told him. "He takes good care of our school and makes sure that everything is in good working condition. He comes early in the morning, while you're still asleep, to make sure that we have a safe and clean building in which to learn. His nights are short, and his days are long."

At about that time, the bell rang, and the children raced out to recess in the schoolyard. Immediately, Mr. Jones stepped into the quiet classroom.

"Hi," the busy custodian said. "I'll be here only a few minutes. I want to take out your trash and pick up a few things while the kids are outside."

"Thank you for all you do," the teacher said. "You do a great job."

"Give the praise to God," Mr. Jones replied, as he continued with his work.

❧

Miss Robinson watched as he hurriedly swept and dusted, trying to finish before the children returned. As he worked, he hummed old-time gospel tunes. Once finished, he didn't hesitate before going to the next room. The teacher stepped outside her door and watched as he made his way down the hall, cleaning everything in sight with enthusiasm.

After recess, when all of the children were back at their desks, Mr. Jones walked down the hallway past their room. The teacher heard the clanging of the keys and realized that although many keys hung from his belt, the greatest key that he carried was the key to the kingdom of God. His example revealed to all what really makes a man important: the love he has for God and his devotion to others is surely the key to happiness and success.

WHATEVER YOU DO, WORK AT IT WITH ALL YOUR HEART, AS WORKING FOR THE LORD, NOT FOR MEN.

COLOSSIANS 3:23

❧ IN GOD'S EYES ❧

In *The Upper Room*, Sandra Palmer Carr describes a touching moment with one of her sons. When her younger son Boyd was four years old, she was rocking him in a high-backed, wooden rocking chair, as was her habit. But this time he was facing her, straddling her lap with his knees bent.

Suddenly, he sat up straight, lifted his head, and stared intensely into her eyes. He became very still, and Sandra stopped rocking. He cupped her face in his little hands and said in a near-whisper, "Mommy, I'm in your eyes."

They stayed that way for several long moments, staring into one another's eyes. The rocking stopped, and the room grew quiet. Then Sandra whispered back, "And I'm in yours." Boyd leaned his head against her contentedly, and they resumed their rocking.

In the days that followed, Boyd would often check to see if his discovery still held true. "Am I still in your eyes, Mommy?" he would ask, reaching up to her. She would pull him close to her so he could look into her eyes and see for himself—he was still there![45]

❧

How can we be assured we are always in God's eyes? The Bible has many, many verses to indicate He is continuously thinking of us, attending to us, and doing all He can to bless us. Certainly, Jesus' death and resurrection are a constant reminder of how dear and precious we are to Him.

One of the best times to stop and see yourself in God's eyes is just before falling asleep. Your Heavenly Father desires to rock you to sleep in His love, letting you stop now and then to call to mind a verse of Scripture that tells you how much you mean to Him.

You should never doubt you are the focus of God's tender care and attention. You can have a grateful and confident heart knowing you are always in His eyes.

THE EYES OF THE LORD
ARE ON THE RIGHTEOUS.

PSALM 34:15

❧ A PRAYER IN THE NIGHT ❧

As the day turned into night, Renee welcomed
the time for rest. Taking her small son to the hospital
to endure a battery of tests had made her day
difficult. Exhaustion had set in, and her nerves were
frayed. While the doctor felt that the test results
would be good, she was still concerned. After putting
the baby into his crib, tears flowed down her face
when she left his room.

The ringing of the telephone startled her.
Before she answered it, she tried to control her tears
but found that it was impossible. When Renee
answered the phone, the caller—a wise woman named
Carol—realized immediately that Renee was upset.
Carol asked if she could pray with her. After she
agreed, Carol prayed the sweetest prayer Renee had
ever heard. Carol then told her that she loved her
and assured her that things would be all right.

As Renee placed the receiver back on the hook,
she had a new outlook regarding her son's health.
Somehow she knew that God had heard every word
that had been spoken during that prayer, as Carol

❧

had interceded with Him to bless Renee's family. She had the assurance that all would be well.

As the sun rose the next morning, Renee awoke with a new sense of peace. Confidently, she dialed the doctor and received wonderful news. All the tests were negative. Her son would be fine.

"Thank God!" she shouted, grateful that He had heard her prayer.

Prayer is the most powerful force in the world. It serves as a direct line to God. It also serves as a time to celebrate happiness and success, giving God the full credit for all of our accomplishments. Prayer is a privilege and a wonderful gift given by a loving God. Day or night, He's always available to listen to every word.

———

THE PRAYER OFFERED IN FAITH
WILL MAKE THE SICK PERSON WELL;
THE LORD WILL RAISE HIM UP.

JAMES 5:15

❧ FAITHFUL TO THE END ❧

For fifty years Sister Agnes and Mrs. Baker had
prayed for their nation of Latvia to be freed from Soviet
oppression. Most of all, they prayed for the freedom to
worship in their Methodist Church in Leipája. When
the atheistic Soviet regime had come into power, the
enemy invaders had taken over their church building
and turned the sanctuary into a sports hall.

Their prayers were answered in 1991, when the
oppression came to an end. The Soviets left, and the
tiny nation was free. But it needed to be rebuilt, and
Sister Agnes and Mrs. Baker were determined to help.

First the two women, now past eighty, talked to a
local minister. They said if he would agree to be their
pastor, they would be his first members. A church
was reborn!

Next they had to regain ownership of the
building. That done, they began getting the church
ready for worship services. One of the church
members undertook painting the twenty-five-foot-
high walls. For weeks, she mounted scaffolding and
painted the walls and ceiling. The tall Palladian
windows were cleaned to a bright, gleaming shine,
and the wood floor was restored to a rich luster.

❧

Because of careful record keeping by church members, the original church pews were found in storage out in the country. They were returned and put into place for worshipers. Sister Agnes had kept the church pump organ safe in her own home, so she returned it to the sanctuary. When she wasn't directing the choir, she played it with great enthusiasm.

God had been faithful! Lenin had predicted Christianity would die out within a generation. After the grandmothers died, he said, there would be no more Christians left. But he didn't know Sister Agnes and Mrs. Baker and the God they loved!

God wants to show Himself strong on your behalf, just as He did for Mrs. Baker and Sister Agnes. Jesus said, "'I will build My church, and the gates of [hell] shall not prevail against it'" (Matthew 16:18 NKJV).

You are part of His Church, and He will not let evil triumph over you! No matter what you are facing tonight, have faith that He will bring you through.

THE EYES OF THE LORD RUN TO
AND FRO THROUGHOUT THE WHOLE
EARTH, TO SHOW HIMSELF STRONG
IN THE BEHALF OF THEM WHOSE
HEART IS PERFECT TOWARD HIM.

2 CHRONICLES 16:9 KJV

John loved to run and walk in the park during the mild winter weather where he lived. So he was surprised one morning in mid-January when he discovered that the area had been covered with a blanket of snow during the night. But since he was up early anyway, John decided to go ahead and run on the graveled jogging trail in the park. No one had been out yet to leave footprints in the snow, but he had been on the trail often enough to know its general direction and its twists and turns. John forged a path along the trail, leaving the prints of his shoes in the snow. After several laps, other joggers joined him on the course, following in his footprints.

Later that day, John returned to the park to walk his dogs. As he walked around the jogging trail, he noticed that the melting snow showed the route of the graveled trail in many places. It differed from the path of footprints. Now that the path was partially visible, people followed it rather than the footprints in the snow.

John thought about the way he lived his life. Most individuals follow an established way rather than forging their own path. It is a unique person who breaks away and makes his own footsteps. Did he know God's pathway well enough to walk it in uncertain circumstances? Did he set a course so that those who followed him would not be misled?

Tonight, ask yourself whether you know God's path for your life. All of us have doubts as we go through life, but if we study God's Word and keep our eyes on Jesus, we can follow in the footsteps of our faith. We can make footprints for those who come after us.[46]

LIFT YOUR DROOPING HANDS
AND STRENGTHEN YOUR WEAK
KNEES, AND MAKE STRAIGHT
PATHS FOR YOUR FEET.

HEBREWS 12:12-13 NRSV

✢ DEEP ROOTS ✢

The root system of bunch grass that grows in the hilly high country is deep, far-reaching, and very extensive. A single plant may have up to seventeen miles of roots growing underground. This sturdy grass withstands the extensive grazing and trampling of livestock and each year puts out new growth.

All year round the bunch grass provides protein for animals. Even when covered by winter snow, it provides rich nutrition for deer, mountain sheep, and range horses. In the fall, its bronze blades provide one of the best nutrition sources available.

People also need vast root systems so their lives can be nourished and provide nourishment for others. Our root system gives us the strength to withstand being "trampled" by the challenges we face every day and the nutrition we need to replenish our resources when we've been "grazed" upon.

What makes up our root system? For most of us, it's family. Our parents and relatives began nurturing us the day we were born. No matter how many miles or years separate us, we turn to them (or to our memory of what they taught us) for wisdom and guidance.

✢

Another part of our root system is people outside the family circle—our friends, coworkers, and people in our church—who have loved us, believed in us, and given us a helping hand as we've struggled to find our place in the world.

More important than all these is our vital connection to God. Even if your family, friends, coworkers, and church forsake you, God will never forsake you. He is the One who knows everything about you and still loves you. He gives you the desires of your heart and has shaped your destiny.

Let your roots grow down deep into the soul of God's loving presence, and He will provide you with nourishment that will overflow into the lives of all those around you.

———

AS YOU RECEIVED CHRIST JESUS THE LORD, SO CONTINUE TO LIVE IN HIM. KEEP YOUR ROOTS DEEP IN HIM AND HAVE YOUR LIVES BUILT ON HIM.

COLOSSIANS 2:6-7 NCV

↜ A SPECIAL NIGHT ↝

As Rebecca's one-year-old son, Dylan, played in the bathtub with his favorite toy—a little sailor—she silently asked God how they should spend the rest of the day. Every day seemed to be the same, a combination of errands and housework.

Dylan grabbed the sailor and plopped him into his boat, splashing water in Rebecca's face. Somehow, the splashing water reminded her that Navy ships had recently docked in their port city. "There are men in those ships!" she shouted.

Rebecca's family always enjoyed visiting the Navy vessels, but this time she sensed God directing them to minister to the six hundred servicemen who had been at sea for the last five months. But how? Rebecca grabbed a towel and her dripping-wet baby and took off to go shopping for the newly arrived sailors.

As night drew near, her family, carrying gifts, climbed aboard a guided missile destroyer. The sailors, eager to see what was inside the green and gold boxes, greeted them. After the command duty officer was summoned on deck to receive their gifts,

↜↝

the officer offered to take Rebecca's family on a private tour.

To their surprise, when they visited the wardroom, they saw that one of the boxes had already been placed at the head of the captain's table. Trying not to notice, Rebecca quickly looked away, staring at a portrait. In the reflection of the glass, she watched an officer take something out of the box. She sensed the Lord whispering to her, *I want them all, so I start at the top.*

Lightly touching the rails, Rebecca's family prayed for each man who would hold that rail during the stormy seas of life. As the sailors lowered the American flag and illuminated the friendship lights, Rebecca's family bid them farewell.

Tonight, ask the Lord how He wants you to spend your tomorrow. Be available for Him. In doing so, you may touch many lives and make new friends.

———

GOD HATH GIVEN THEE ALL THEM THAT SAIL WITH THEE.

ACTS 27:24 KJV

⤙ TAKE CONTROL OF ANGER ⤚

One of the most controversial events in America occurred when Bernard Goetz had enough and decided he wasn't going to take it anymore. He did what many people have wanted to do—he fought back and pulled a gun when he was attacked on the subway.

Goetz's action received an outpouring of support. He touched a nerve in people who have simply had enough of other people threatening their lives. Criticism comes, however, when we allow guns to be in the hands of angry, violent people. As Christians, anger can be a terrible enemy.

The beginnings of anger almost go unnoticed: petty irritations, ordinary frustrations, minor aggravations—things we experience daily. Then these small things start adding up. Pressures build and turn into rage. Without relief, pent-up anger can turn violent with devastating consequences.

How do we keep our passions from becoming uncontrolled anger? How should we defuse the anger that makes us want to retaliate?

There is a righteous, Godly anger that energizes us to action, to right the wrong, to defend the innocent. However, anger becomes sin when it turns to hate and retribution. Then it is often expressed in

⤙⤚

inappropriate, destructive ways. We can fly off the handle and act in ways that are as hurtful as what caused us to be angry in the first place. Worse yet, we can store up anger and become bitter and resentful.

An old proverb says, "He who goes angry to bed has the devil for a bedfellow." This is not a condition for sweet sleep!

There are several things we can do to take control of our anger before it takes control of us:

1. Yell at God first! He already knows you're upset.
2. Ask God to give you understanding about the situation, to show you the root of your anger, if that's the case.
3. Turn the situation over to God. Forgive those who have hurt you, and let Him deal with them. Turn His power loose in the circumstances.
4. Don't do anything without having complete inner peace from His Spirit.

Then you can sleep easily at night, knowing God can turn anything around to work for your good.

BE YE ANGRY, AND SIN NOT:
LET NOT THE SUN GO DOWN
UPON YOUR WRATH.

EPHESIANS 4:26 KJV

The Garden of Gethsemane seemed darker that night. During the day, visitors sat in the shade of its olive trees beside slow, trickling creeks to behold the beauty of desert flowers. It was a place of rest—a sanctuary for those who were weary.

But that night its beauty brought Jesus no peace or tranquility. On worn knees He knelt down, doubled over in despair for that which He knew was soon to come. As He clenched His hands, His soul cried out to God. The intensity of his agonizing prayer forced droplets of blood through his skin to bead upon His brow. Facing sure death by crucifixion, He asked of His Heavenly Father, *Must it come to this?* But in the hour of decision, He prayed, *Nevertheless, not my will but thine be done.*

It's comforting to know that when we dread tomorrow, our Lord knows exactly how we feel. He knows what it's like to be a father who takes a job he may dislike because it helps him put food on the table for his children. He knows what it's like to be falsely accused and wind up in court facing a judge and jury. He knows what it's like to be on the road and lose someone you love back home.

Because Jesus Christ endured this suffering for us, willingly accepting His fate, we have His assurance that He is always with us. He will never leave us or forsake us. For a hope in the heavenly life to come for us, He was willing to be the final sacrifice.

The end of His story is not found in the terrible beatings, the crown of thorns, the ridicule of an angry mob, or being nailed to the cross. The victory is that He died and was resurrected. His triumph is an empty tomb.

So tonight, whatever you're facing tomorrow, know that God will be walking through it with you. Lean on Him.

I RECKON THAT THE SUFFERINGS OF THIS PRESENT TIME ARE NOT WORTHY TO BE COMPARED WITH THE GLORY WHICH SHALL BE REVEALED IN US.

ROMANS 8:18 KJV

❧ EVENING OF PEACE ❧

In the book of Genesis, each day of creation is concluded with the phrase, *and there was evening, and there was morning.*

From the Hebrew perspective, the day begins at evening, specifically with the setting of the sun. This is unlike our Western tradition, where we start our days at the crack of dawn and consider night to be the end of a long day.

What does it mean for the day to begin at evening?

For Hebrew people throughout the centuries, the transition from afternoon to evening has been marked by prayer. "Evening prayer" is a Jewish custom. After prayer, families gather together for a meal.

The most holy day of the week, the Sabbath, begins with the lighting of candles and a proclamation of faith, then a more formal family dinner. After the evening meal, Jewish families traditionally gather together to read God's Word and discuss how His laws apply to their lives. The evening ends in rest.

Consider the priorities evidenced by their way of life:

First, there is a focus upon prayer and one's relationship with God.

Second, there is an emphasis on family life.

Third, a daily study of Scripture makes God's Word the last thought of the day.

Fourth, rest and sleep.

It was only after a Hebrew talked with God, enjoyed the love and fellowship of family, studied the Scriptures, and rested, that work was undertaken.

What would happen in your life if you adopted this strategy for your evening hours? Is it possible you would find yourself more renewed and refreshed, more energetic and healthy, more creative and productive? Might the priorities you desire in your life become a reality?

Why not give it a try? Begin your next day in the evening, and wake up knowing you're totally refreshed—spirit, soul, and body—to have a full and productive day!

THERE WAS EVENING, AND THERE WAS MORNING—THE FIRST DAY.

GENESIS 1:5

⚘ TOO BUSY ⚘

Patricia had a habit of ignoring others whenever she was particularly busy. One evening her husband complained, "I feel like yesterday's diapers." Patricia told him that she was simply busy and didn't mean to treat him badly, but as she fell asleep that night she thought about what he had said. Had she been ignoring him?

She thought about her busy days filled with changing diapers, grocery shopping, laundry, taking the twins to soccer practice, school plays, parent-teacher meetings, and volunteer work. She felt exhausted just thinking about it. Brushing off her husband's concerns, she dropped into a deep sleep.

Then one day she discovered for herself just how he felt. She had dropped by the offices of a well-known organization to leave some information. She had hoped to meet and talk with some of the volunteers, but to Patricia's surprise everyone was too busy to speak with her. Convinced that she was not welcome, she left in discouragement. That incident, however, made her realize how her husband felt, and she vowed to spend more time listening to him and being there for him.

⚘

In our busy world, we often ignore one another. Many of us are overworked and overextended, and we find that it's easy to make a habit of ignoring others, including those we love the most. But we can make a difference in the lives of the people around us by taking the time to listen to them—by showing them that they are precious to God, and to us.

Jesus Christ said that the greatest commandment of all is to love one another, and that His followers would be known by their love—a deep and abiding love. So tomorrow, as you go about your day, take a moment from your busyness. Make a call and tell a friend that you think she's special. Not only will you brighten up your friend's day, you'll also speak volumes to a hurting and neglected world.

THESE THINGS I COMMAND YOU,
THAT YE LOVE ONE ANOTHER.

JOHN 15:17 KJV

TRUE FULFILLMENT

Fulfillment is something for which every person seems to long. In its simplest meaning, fulfillment refers to being "fully filled"—having a complete sense of accomplishment.

If you lack a sense of fulfillment at day's end, ask yourself, *What did I not do that I felt I should have done?* You'll be calling into question your values, priorities, and goals. As you see areas in which you have fallen short, ask the Lord to help you discipline yourself to achieve what you know is good, adjust your priorities and goals, and refine your values.

A lack of fulfillment isn't the fault of circumstances or another person's behavior. It is a matter of your outer life being in harmony with your inner life, living outwardly what you profess with your mouth and believe in your heart.

For Robert Louis Stevenson, this was the definition of a successful life:

> "That man is a success who has lived well, laughed often and loved much; who has gained the respect of intelligent men and the love of children; who has filled his niche and

accomplished his task; who leaves the world better than he found it, whether by an improved poppy, a perfect poem, or a rescued soul; who never lacked appreciation of earth's beauty or failed to express it; who looked for the best in others and gave the best he had."[47]

Do you have a definition of success against which to gauge your own sense of fulfillment?

There's still time to make today fulfilling. Take a moment to reflect upon your goals, priorities, and values. Ask the Lord to show you where they may need some adjusting. As you rethink these important issues, you will be filled with the knowledge that true fulfillment comes in simply knowing and obeying Him.

"I HAVE COME THAT THEY MAY HAVE LIFE, AND THAT THEY MAY HAVE IT MORE ABUNDANTLY."

JOHN 10:10 NKJV

❧ NIGHT BLOOMERS ❧

Some of the most fragrant flowers in the garden stay tightly closed, or "sleep," during the day. They open only later in the afternoon and evening, perfuming the night air with their sweet scents.

The most magnificent of these late bloomers is the moonflower. Moonflowers look like white morning glories, except that their blossoms are enormous—up to eight inches across. Each bloom lasts for only one night, but the scent more than makes up for the short performance.[48] Just as nature lends itself to day and night creations, so there are "morning people" who feel their best in the early hours of the day and "night people" who seem to bloom after dark. If you are a late bloomer, fill the night air with the sweet fragrance of prayer before God this evening.

The Lord looks forward to your companionship and is waiting to hear from you. Give Him your attention and listen to what He wants to tell you. Treat God as you would a dear friend.

Review your schedule to find time you can commit to God. Have no time? You may be

❧

overlooking some ready-made times, such as your drive to and from work or your coffee break. Find a place of isolation without distractions.

Jesus said, "Enter your closet" (Matthew 6:6). This "closet" can be any place, any time you can be alone with Him. Or you may want to designate one special place where you pray.

As you spend time seeking God during the night, you will bring a sweet fragrance into the throne room of God. The Bible describes this beautifully in Revelation 8:3 KJV: "And another angel came and stood at the altar, having a golden censer; and there was given unto him much incense, that he should offer it with the prayers of all saints upon the golden altar which was before the throne."

Enjoy your night glories.

───────

LET MY PRAYER BE SET FORTH
BEFORE THEE AS INCENSE; AND
THE LIFTING UP OF MY HANDS
AS THE EVENING SACRIFICE.

PSALM 141:2 KJV

❧ JOY IN THE JOURNEY ❧

Sometimes it seems as if life is lived backwards! When we are young and have only a limited perspective, we have to make huge decisions in life that will shape the rest of our years. But we can—and are wise to—learn from those who have gained insight from life's experiences.

In a sociological study, fifty people over the age of ninety-five were asked the question: If you could live your life over again, what would you do differently? Three general responses emerged from the questionnaire.

If I had to do it over again. . .

↪ *I would reflect more.*

↪ *I would risk more.*

↪ *I would do more things that would live on after I am dead.*[49]

An elderly woman wrote this about how she would live her life if she had it to live over again:

"I'd make more mistakes next time; I'd relax; I would limber up; I would be sillier than I have been on this trip; I would take fewer things seriously; I would take more chances; I would climb more mountains and swim more rivers; I would eat more ice cream and less beans; I would perhaps have more actual troubles, but I'd have fewer imaginary ones.

"You see, I'm one of those people who lives sensibly and sanely hour after hour, day after day. Oh, I've had my moments, and if I had it to do over again, I'd have more of them. In fact, I'd try to do nothing else, just moments, one after the other, instead of living so many years ahead of time."[50]

Listen and learn! Life cannot be all work and no play, yet you want your life to be meaningful, to God, to your loved ones who follow you, and to yourself.

Reflect on your life tonight. Ask God to show you the true meaning of your existence, what you are to accomplish—and how to have fun along the way!

———

INCLINE YOUR EAR TO WISDOM,
AND APPLY YOUR HEART
TO UNDERSTANDING.

PROVERBS 2:2 NKJV

❧ WORKING THE ❧
NIGHT SHIFT

As a nurse, Linda had worked the day shift for years. When her supervisor changed her schedule to the night shift, Linda thought, *No problem.*

It wasn't long, however, before Linda discovered she had a hard time getting to sleep during the day. Then, after several hours or more of trying to fall asleep, when she finally drifted off, her telephone or doorbell often would ring and wake her.

Linda would return to bed only to toss and turn throughout the day, trying to find a comfortable sleeping position. So when evening arrived and it was time for her to go to work, Linda would be exhausted.

She knew she had to do something so she could get enough sleep. She hooked up an answering machine to the phone and placed a "Please do not disturb" sign on the door. Even so, the ringing phone still woke her, and aggressive door-to-door salespeople ignored the sign on the door. No matter what she tried, nothing seemed to work.

Then one day she read Psalm 127 NKJV. "I read the scripture, and I knew the *He* in verse 2 was God and *His beloved* was me," Linda said. "So I started saying that verse when I got into bed during the day to go to sleep. And soon I'd be sound asleep."

As the days passed, the same thing happened over and over. Linda would recite the verse, think about it for a while, and drift into sleep. Today, she has no problem sleeping during the day as she manages her evening work shift and personal family life.

When you go to bed tonight or tomorrow morning, think about that verse. God has promised that He will give you, His beloved, the rest you need. Claim His promise!

———

UNLESS THE LORD BUILDS THE HOUSE, THEY LABOR IN VAIN WHO BUILD IT; UNLESS THE LORD GUARDS THE CITY, THE WATCHMAN STAYS AWAKE IN VAIN. IT IS VAIN FOR YOU TO RISE UP EARLY, TO SIT UP LATE, TO EAT THE BREAD OF SORROWS; FOR SO HE GIVES HIS BELOVED SLEEP.

PSALM 127:1-2 NKJV

✌ REST IN FREEDOM ✌

James Forten, a fifteen-year-old slave, served in the American Revolution as a powder boy aboard the American privateer *Royal Louis,* a small ship commanded by Stephen Decatur Sr. When offered his freedom and a life of ease in England, the young sailor from Philadelphia replied, "No, I'm a prisoner for my country, and I'll never be a traitor to her."

The struggle for freedom did not leave any lingering doubts in his mind. But some slaves must have questioned it; after all, they were slaves—the property of others. Why should they fight for liberty—for independence and freedom? Freedom for whom? If James had any doubts, though, they were drowned out by his belief that the Revolution was a path to freedom—for all men.

Along with thousands of other slaves, Forten endured tremendous hardship for many months during the war. Finally, after being set free, he became an inventor and manufacturer, giving much of his wealth to aid poor and struggling blacks, and a founder of the abolition movement, with the hope of ending slavery in America. Forten's faith, courage, grit, and perseverance helped bring a new, free nation into being.[51]

Many people today are still enslaved. The dark chains of pornography, drugs, tobacco, and alcohol keep them in bondage. For others, physical or emotional abuse holds them in shackles.

But Jesus Christ can free you from the chains that may be holding you in bondage. Jesus invites you, "'Come unto me, all ye that labour and are heavy laden, and I will give you rest. Take my yoke upon you, and learn of me; for I am meek and lowly in heart: and ye shall find rest unto your souls'" (Matthew 11:28-29 KJV). Find freedom in Christ today.

———

MY YOKE IS EASY, AND
MY BURDEN IS LIGHT.

MATTHEW 11:30 KJV

REFERENCES

ENDNOTES

1. Kathleen Lowthert. Adapted from *The Upper Room,* January 29, 1999.

2. *Newsweek,* January 22, 1996, p. 14.

3. *A Diary of Readings,* John Baillie (NY: Collier Books, Macmillan Publishing Co., 1955), Day 202.

4. *A Moment a Day,* Mary Beckwith and Kathi Mills, ed. (Ventura, CA: Regal Books, 1988), p. 247.

5. Adapted from *Daily Wisdom,* January 26, 1999.

6. *Silent Strength,* Lloyd John Ogilvie (Eugene, OR: Harvest House, 1990), p. 129.

7. *Illustrations Unlimited,* James S. Hewett, ed. (Wheaton: Tyndale House, 1988), p. 25.

8. *American Health,* April 1996, pp. 76-78.

9. Diane Rayner, *The Best Stories from Guideposts.* (Wheaton, IL: Tyndale House Publishers, 1987), pp. 219-222.

10. *Scientific American,* July 1995, pp. 60-64.

11. Nanette Thorsen-Snipes, *Southern Lifestyles,* Summer 1996, p. 38.

12. *The Treasure Chest,* Brian Culhane, ed. (San Francisco: Harper Collins, 1995), p. 146.

13. Nanette Thorsen-Snipes, *Christian Reader,* December 1999.

14. *The Treasure Chest,* Brian Culhane, ed. (San Francisco: Harper Collins, 1995), p. 109.

15. Ibid, p. 94.

16. *Jewish Wisdom,* Rabbi Joseph Telushkin (NY: William Morrow and Company, Inc., 1994), pp. 182-184.

17. *The World's Best Religious Quotations,* James Gilchrist Lawson, ed. (NY: Fleming H. Revell Company, 1930), p. 99.

18. Kelly McHugh. Adapted from *The Upper Room,* January-February, 1999. January 9, 1999.

19. *The Treasure Chest,* Brian Culhane, ed. (San Francisco: Harper Collins, 1995), p. 92.

20. George Prins. Adapted from *Daily Wisdom,* January 29, 1999.

21. *The Treasury of Inspirational Quotations & Illustrations,* E. Paul Hovey, ed. (Grand Rapids, MI: Baker Books, 1994), p. 168.

22. *Creative Living,* Summer 1993, p. 26.

23. *The Treasure Chest,* Brian Culhane, ed. (San Francisco: Harper Collins, 1995), p. 88.

24. Ibid, p. 56.

25. *Amazing Grace,* Kenneth W. Osbeck (Grand Rapids, MI: Kregel Publications, 1993), p. 228.

26. Ibid, p. 49.

27. *Creative Living,* Autumn 1995, pp. 20-24.

[28] *Encyclopedia of 7,700 Illustrations*, Paul Lee Tan (Garland, TX: Bible Communications Inc., 1979), p. 1387.

[29] *You Don't Have to Be Blind to See*, Jim Stovall (Nashville, TN: Thomas Nelson Publishers, 1996), p. 90.

[30] *The Joy of Working*, Dennis Waitley and Reni L. Witt (NY: Dodd, Mead & Company, 1985), pp. 213-214.

[31] *Knight's Master Book of 4,000 Illustrations*, Walter B.Knight, (Grand Rapids, MI: Eerdmans Publishing Co., 1956), p. 448.

[32] Ibid.

[33] *A Moment a Day*, Mary Beckwith and Kathi Mills, ed. (Ventura, CA: Regal Books, 1988), p. 174.

[34] *Newsweek*, November 27, 1995, pp. 62-63.

[35] *101 More Hymn Stories*, Kenneth W. Osbeck (Grand Rapids, MI: Kregel Publications, 1985), pp. 24-26.

[36] *The Best-Loved Poems of the American People*, selected by Hazel Felleman (New York: Doubleday, 1936), p. 305.

[37] *It Is Well with My Soul*, Horatio Gates Spafford, 1873.

[38] *A Moment a Day*, Mary Beckwith and Kathi Mille, ed., (Ventura, CA: Regal Books, 1988), p. 25.

[39] *Look Out Fear, Here Comes Faith!*, Marion Bond West. (Ann Arbor, MI: Servant Publications, 1991), pp. 155-158.

[40] *Decision*, March 1996, p. 33.

[41] *Unto the Hills: A Devotional Treasury*, Billy Graham (Waco, TX: Word Books, 1986), p. 223.

[42] Jason Cheng. Adapted from *The Upper Room*, January-February 1999. January 22, 1999.

[43] *Spiritual Fitness*, Doris Donnelly (NY: Harper-San Francisco, A Division of HarperCollins, 1993) pp. 155-56, 165-66.

[44] *The New Yorker*, November 20, 1995, pp. 56-57, 59, 62-64.

[45] *The Upper Room*, May-June 1996, p.15.

[46] Adapted from *The Upper Room*, January-February, 1999. January 30, 1999.

[47] *The Treasure Chest*, Brian Culhane, ed. (San Francisco: Harper Collins, 1995), p. 10.

[48] *Tales of the Shimmering Sky*, Susan Milord (Charlotte, VT: Williamson Publishing, 1996), p. 47.

[49] "Who Switched the Price Tags?" Tony Campolo, *The Inspirational Study Bible*, Max Lucado, ed., (Dallas: Word Publishing, 1995) p. 402.

[50] *Illustrations Unlimited*, James W. Hewett, ed. (Wheaton: Tyndale House, 1988) pp. 25-26.

[51] *Black Heroes of the American Revolution*, Burke Davis. (New York: Harcourt Brace Jovanovich, 1976), p. 23.

Also available from Honor Books:
Good Morning, God!

If you have enjoyed this book,
or if it has impacted your life,
we would like to hear from you.

Please contact us at:

Honor Books
An Imprint of Cook Communications Ministries
4050 Lee Vance View
Colorado Springs, CO 80918
Or by e-mail at cookministries.com